OUR HEART PSALMS

30 Interactive Devotions Based on the
Psalms of Scripture
with Optional Journal Prompts

Joyce K. Ellis

OUR HEART PSALMS BY JOYCE K. ELLIS
Straight Street Books is an imprint of LPCBooks
a division of Iron Stream Media
100 Missionary Ridge, Birmingham, AL 35242

ISBN: 978-1-64526-270-1
Copyright © 2020 by Joyce K. Ellis
Cover Design by Hannah Linder
Interior Design by AtriTex Technologies P Ltd.

Available in print from your local bookstore, online, or from the publisher at ShopLPC.com.

For more information on this book and the author, visit www.joycekellis.com.

All rights reserved. Noncommercial interests may reproduce portions of this book without the express written permission of LPCBooks, provided the text does not exceed 500 words. When reproducing text from this book, include the following credit line: "*Our Heart Psalms* by Joyce K. Ellis published by LPCBooks. Used by permission."

Commercial interests: No part of this publication may be reproduced in any form, stored in a retrieval system, or transmitted in any form by any means—electronic, photocopy, recording, or otherwise—without prior written permission of the publisher, except as provided by the United States of America copyright law.

Unless otherwise indicated, all Scripture quotations are taken from the *Holy Bible, New Living Translation*, copyright © 1996, 2004, 2015 by Tyndale House Foundation. Used by permission of Tyndale House Publishers, Inc., Carol Stream, Illinois 60188. All rights reserved.

Scriptures marked as (GNT) are taken from the *Good News Translation* – Second Edition © 1992 by American Bible Society. Used by permission.

Scripture quotations marked (HCSB) are taken from the *Holman Christian Standard Bible®*, Copyright © 1999, 2000, 2002, 2003, 2009 by Holman Bible Publishers. Used by permission. Holman Christian Standard Bible®, Holman CSB®, and HCSB® are federally registered trademarks of Holman Bible Publishers.

Scripture quotations marked MSG are taken from *The Message* by Eugene H. Peterson, copyright © 1993, 1994, 1995, 1996, 2000, 2001, 2002. Used by permission of NavPress Publishing Group. All rights reserved.

All web addresses (URLs) cited in this book are offered solely as a resource to the reader. The citation of these websites does not in any way imply an endorsement on the part of the author or the publisher, nor does the author or publisher vouch for their content for the life of this book.

Brought to you by the creative team at LPCBooks:
(LPCBooks.com):
Eddie Jones, Cindy Sproles, Denise Loock

Library of Congress Cataloging-in-Publication Data
Ellis, Joyce K.
Our Heart Psalms / Joyce K. Ellis Title / 1st ed.
Printed in the United States of America

Praise for OUR HEART PSALMS

Our Heart Psalms is a journey deeper. This helpful devotional will take you deeper into the Word, deeper into yourself, and deeper into the heart of God. If you want to read, understand, and reflect on the meaning of the Psalms of Scripture, let Joyce Ellis be your guide.

~Lawrence W. Wilson
Author of *Promises and Prayers for Men*

Our Heart Psalms is a refreshing, honest exploration of the Psalms of Scripture. Author Joyce Ellis allows us into her personal life as she sought to find her path through the challenges and joys of her life. As she turned to the Psalms for support, she found strength, hope, and an unexpected closeness to God. *Our Heart Psalms* is a must-read for all who choose to walk with God.

~Elizabeth Levang, PhD
Grief counselor
Author of *Remembering with Love*
and *When Men Grieve*

Joyce Ellis has given us a wonderful gift in her book, *Our Heart Psalms*. Joyce has the unique ability to bring her readers on an interactive journey that I believe changes the depth of their walk with

God. The psalmists of old expressed their worship to God through psalms. These psalms were full of emotion but never ceased to reveal the truth of who God is. Joyce teaches us how to do the same thing. Grounding her devotions in Scripture, Joyce uses her engaging storytelling and beautifully written modern psalms to guide her readers into the practice of writing their own psalms of worship to God. Take thirty days to work through this book. You may never be the same again!

~**Brian Schulenburg**
Discipleship pastor
Wooddale Church
Eden Prairie, MN

I chuckled, marveled, and wept my way through Joyce Ellis's delightfully frank devotional book based on the Psalms. Using abundant examples, helpful tips, and a variety of structural options, she gently guides her readers into fresh ways of connecting with the Almighty. Believers new to the faith, seasoned Christians, and readers with troubled pasts will all discover how freeing it can be to speak their mind to a God who understands and cares.

~**Sharon Sheppard**
Crisis pregnancy counselor

If you have been looking for a devotional book that is clear, concise, and easy to read yet full of biblical truths and guidance for everyday living, Joyce Ellis's *Our Heart Psalms* is just that book. Joyce has the ability to shape her words in such a way that they reach out to every reader. Her sincere spirit and love for Jesus Christ shine through on every page, and her insights will spur you on in your faith journey. I cannot recommend this little gem enough.

~Dr. David Donelson
Pastor of Care and Traditional Worship
Wooddale Church

I have always believed that we write ourselves to health, wholeness, and happiness by writing back to God those truths He first shared with our hearts. In *Our Heart Psalms* you have the opportunity to learn and process precious truths about God, see beautiful sentiments written by author Joyce Ellis, then pick up a pen and create. Open this book and find a renewed love for the Psalms, for the Lord, and for writing!

~Pam Farrel
Author of 50 books
Coauthor of *Discovering Hope in the Psalms*

Joyce K. Ellis's practical devotional book, *Our Heart Psalms*, draws out our longings and pain and draws us to God. Through heartfelt stories and Scripture, these interactive devotions invite us to turn our praise to God with our own personal psalms that refocus our hearts. Beautifully composed, this stirring book invites us into life.

>~Jane Rubietta
>Speaker
>Author of *Worry Less So You Can Live More*

As I read *Our Heart Psalms* by Joyce Ellis, I thought of conversations with students in a class on prayer, when I guide them through the psalmists' dialogues with God. I remembered my own psalm therapy, when prayerful journaling helped me face my personal valleys and shadows of death as I battle brain damage and epilepsy. I nodded at Joyce's phrases, knowing her own deep love for the Listener of our prayers. I remembered honest conversations I have enjoyed with Joyce as we knew the Shepherd was with us. Joyce is a gifted writer and spiritual director. She cares deeply. I invite you to open your eyes, your mind, and your heart to *Our Heart Psalms*. I believe the Great Shepherd will lead you beside still waters and restore your soul.

>~Chris Maxwell
>Campus pastor at Emmanuel College in Georgia
>Author of *Underwater: When Encephalitis, Brain Injury and Epilepsy Change Everything*

If you think *Our Heart Psalms* is simply another devotional on the book of Psalms, think again. Joyce Ellis makes the case that each one of us is designed to be a psalm-writer. Her own experiences with this practice prove how life-changing it can be. These interactive devotions will help you understand your own heart better. Best of all, as you relate to God on a deeper level of honesty and trust, you will come to understand His heart more fully as well.

~Dianne Neal Matthews
Author of *The One Year Women of the Bible* devotional guide

Our Heart Psalms is a magnificent devotional that journeys with you through the book of Psalms in an authentic way. Joyce has done a superb job in helping readers to do their heart work. I believe everyone needs to take this journey of ascent and descent as one discovers that God can handle anything we say or feel. Get ready to know the creator God as well as yourself in an intimate way.

~Donna Fagerstrom
Author, Speaker, Musician

In this inspirational volume, Joyce Ellis has skillfully and uniquely transposed the hymn and prayer book of ancient Israel to help us thrive in the daily challenges of our modern lives. Through her own personal stories and helpful journal prompts she provides a most useful guide to practically and personally engaging the Psalms to express our deepest longings and highest praise to our wonderful God. This book will bless you at whatever level you engage it, from simply reading it as a devotional to responding to every practical suggestion.

~Roy Kruse
Bible teacher

For those of us seeking an ever-growing intimacy with our Lord, it's a beautiful thing to encounter new and fresh tools that assist in that quest. In her devotional, *Our Heart Psalms*, Joyce Ellis draws from real-life illustrations, as well as scriptural and current psalms to prompt, guide, and encourage us, as intimacy seekers, in identifying and expressing our own innermost thoughts to the One who loves us the most.

~Heidi Satterberg
Speaker and Musician

Our Heart Psalms is the antidote for a prayer life that is in a rut or needs a shot of adrenaline. Joyce K. Ellis's fresh approach to praying like the psalmists is vulnerable, honest, encouraging, and practical. Her devotions, journal prompts, and examples of modern psalms will help you channel your emotions into biblical patterns of talking with God on a deeper level.

~Lin Johnson
Editor, Writer, Conference teacher
Director of the Write-to-Publish Conference

CONTENTS

How to Use This Book: Start Where You Are..........*xix*

Section I. VULNERABILITY 1
1. Prelude: Channel Those Feelings 5
2. Remember to Remember 13
3. Release the Pressure Valve 23
4. Navigate the Swells of Emotion 31

Section II. FEELINGS 37
5. Feeling Happy 41
6. Feeling Fearful 47
7. Feeling Depressed 55
8. Feeling Awed by God's Creation 65
9. Feeling Grateful for Who God Is 75
10. Feeling Insecure 85
11. Feeling Joyful 93
12. Feeling Pain 103
13. Feeling Impatient 113
14. Feeling Grateful for What God Has Done 123
15. Feeling Worried 133
16. Feeling Worshipful 143
17. Feeling Attacked 151
18. Feeling Angry 161

19. Feeling Doubtful 171
20. Feeling Grateful for What We Have......179
21. Feeling My Sin...189
22. Feeling Remorseful 199
23. Feeling Unforgiven.......................................209
24. Feeling Like a Failure...................................219
25. Feeling Hopeful...229

Section III. TIMELY, TIMELESS PRAISE......237
26. Accepting the Way God Made Me........239
27. Intimacy with My Creator 249
28. A Sacrifice of Praise.....................................259
29. The A to Z of Praise....................................269
30. Postlude: Joining Timely,
    Timeless Praise..281

Appendix 289

Notes...293

Acknowledgments

My heartfelt thanks to

- Dr. David Glock (Emmaus Bible College, Iowa), in memoriam, for helping me find my voice in the patterns of the Psalms and for inspiring this long-in-the-making book
- Dr. Ardel Caneday (University of Northwestern, St. Paul), who shepherded me through an independent study of the book of Psalms
- Dr. Theron Young (Australian College of Christian Studies), who read early drafts and added helpful comments
- the women and men who worked through some of this material as a Bible study, gave insightful feedback, and contributed psalms of their own to this book
- Cyle Young and the Hartline Literary Agency, for their part in making the connections necessary to bring this project to fruition
- Cindy Sproles, Eddie Jones, and the entire staff of Lighthouse Publishing of the Carolinas, who believed in my heart's desire for this book and took a chance on getting it into print

- Denise Loock for her encouragement and painstaking editing work, helping me communicate more clearly and accurately
- Hannah Thoelke for her fact-checking help with resources
- my husband, Steve, for his love, prayers, support, encouragement, proofreading skills, and extra work to free up time for me to work on this project
- the Lord Jesus Christ for longing to have an honest, intimate relationship with me and with each of His followers.

For all who want to develop
a deeper intimacy with God
and are willing to invest the time to do so

*Once the joy of intimacy with
God has been experienced,
life becomes unbearable
without it.*[1]
—J. Oswald Sanders

Want to dig deeper?

Find tools for further study of the elements of biblical psalms (and ways their patterns can help us shape our own psalms) at Joyce Ellis's website: www.joycekellis.com.

Psalm of My Heart

Sing praise to the Lord of all the earth,
Sing praise to our God of love,
His mercies refresh like gentle rain,
His grace sparkles bright like lakes of diamonds,
His kindness unfolds
As our weakness is showing.
Sing praise to our God of love.
—Joyce K. Ellis

HOW TO USE THIS BOOK:
Start Where You Are

Did you ever try to pray—but couldn't?

In one Ziggy cartoon, the adorable pudgy character stood in front of a sign with a map, such as you would find on a hiking trail or shopping mall. A large arrow pointed to a particular location, labeled, "You are here." Then the sarcastic map instructions accuse poor Ziggy of having no one to blame for it but himself.

That may or may not be true in your experience. We know that the good and the bad in our lives result from our own choices *sometimes*. However, we also know what it's like to suffer the consequences of someone else's negligence, mistakes, unwise choices, or downright evil actions. We also have an Enemy, constantly on the prowl, *looking for anyone he can devour* (1 Peter 5:8 HCSB).

Regardless, we stand, like Ziggy, before a life map that says, "You are here." And perhaps a kinder map would ask, "Where do you want to go?"

Our loving heavenly Father wants each of us to get to know Him intimately. He wants our friendship with Him to be so intimate that we can share every detail of every day with Him: the good, the bad, the ugly—and the beautiful.

Years ago, someone taught me that our prayers should always begin with adoration, praising God. Many days I tried but couldn't. I couldn't tell God how wonderful He is because I was hurting too much, confusion reigned, or anger threatened to erupt. I tried to muster some type of praise, but I felt hypocritical.

However, I noticed that the psalm writers didn't always begin with praise. Some psalms contain no praise at all. But many do, and the resulting praise rising out of the pain honored God all the more.

God has been teaching me to start where I am and work through each situation with Him as I journal my deepest emotions—sometimes from "the pits" to the pinnacles of praise.

Our Heart Psalms invites you to journey with me as I'm still learning how to be completely open and honest with our Creator—who knows everything about us anyway. We'll look at several types of psalms in Scripture and learn how to adopt their patterns, nurturing our intimacy with Him.

This devotional book is designed to be an interactive journal. But feel free to read through the devotions and come back later to journal.

OUR HEART PSALMS

You may find it helpful to begin with Section I—the first four devotions—to become grounded in the concept of vulnerability before God. Then each day following, pick and choose what interests you: **start where you are**.

Section II covers a gamut of emotions, such as joy, happiness (they're not the same), fear, depression, gratitude, and more.

Section III brings everything full circle in an overview of our highest privilege—knowing our God intimately and praising Him, from a heart full of love, for all He is and all He has done for us.

Again, start where you are. On the journal lines provided, write what you're feeling, and start shaping your own psalms. Later you may want to copy them into a bound book as an encouragement for yourself—and a legacy for others.

You may also find the patterns and examples of contemporary psalms (included throughout) helpful in writing psalms of your own. Some examples are mine. Others are from people who have worked through the principles in this book. You may find yourself praying along with them because you can empathize.

While reading *Our Heart Psalms*, read the psalms of Scripture as well. If you invest time doing that—and writing out your own psalms—you'll be amazed how freeing it can be in developing intimacy with God.

Exaltation
A praise psalm

Oh how great it is to praise our gracious God!
My heart thrills to join His people, sing His praise.
Our praise is sweet in His ears
when we lift Him up,
glorifying Jesus Christ, our Savior, Lord,
each in his own language,
each in his own way,
singing praise to the God who makes us one.
Oh how great it is to praise our gracious God!
—Joyce K. Ellis

*O my people, trust in him
at all times.
Pour out your heart to him,
for God is our refuge.*
—Psalm 62:8

I

VULNERABILITY

God longs for us to be open,
honest, and vulnerable.
In response,
He allows us the privilege
of a deeper, more intimate
relationship
with Him.
—Joyce K. Ellis

Wherever You Are

The psalm writer Asaph wrote, *I cry out to God without holding back* (Psalm 77:1).[2]

King David taught that principle as well. Eugene Peterson paraphrases it this way:

> *Never hide your feelings from him.*
> —Psalm 34:5 (MSG)

No matter what pain or joy we're feeling, God delights when we honestly express our emotions to Him. Feel free to read these devotions without following the journal prompts. But journaling your thoughts and emotions may take you to a deeper relationship with the Lord.

*Thoughts disentangle themselves
over the lips and through
the fingertips.*[3]
—Charles R. Swindoll

1

PRELUDE: CHANNEL THOSE FEELINGS

*Please listen and answer me,
for I am overwhelmed by my troubles.*
—Psalm 55:2

"They think my dad had a heart attack." My nephew Ray relayed the message that Sunday afternoon in 1994. Jeanne and Bob (we called him Willie) were driving back to Minneapolis from a weekend in Iowa.

My husband, Steve, and I jumped into our car and headed south, barreling through a dull gray, overcast dusk that mirrored our mood. "Please, dear Lord, don't let him die, please, Lord," I pled continuously. I probably added a perfunctory "Thy will be done" phrase, but I'm not sure I meant it if I did. Willie was only fifty-four, the father of four—the youngest, a son, only thirteen.

Jeanne and Willie had kids about the same ages as ours. We served together in the same inner-city church for many years and worked at the same Bible camp together. We often played table games together into the wee hours of the morning, laughed a lot together, and dreamed of someday RV-ing our way through retirement together.

But that dream evaporated. By the time Steve and I reached the small-town hospital, Willie was gone. I wrapped my arms around Jeanne and cried with her. At the age of forty-eight, my sister became a widow.

Grief seemed to swallow us whole. For months, I dragged around a heavy heart. My own grief intensified as I watched someone I loved so much struggle to regain her bearings. Jeanne kept saying, "I feel like I'm walking around in a fog."

Perhaps in a fog of my own, I couldn't make sense of anything. Such conflicting emotions: Excruciating sorrow that we'd never see him again until we get to heaven. Reluctant joy that he now sat in the presence of the Lord he loved. Anger that God took him so young.

I couldn't process my grief. The pain blurred my nearsighted vision. And the pain wouldn't go away. I kept looking for the *all things* that are supposed to *work together for ... good*, but none showed up (Romans 8:28 HCSB).

The following July, we muddled through our first year without Willie at the helm of the camp where we had seen scores of young people begin or strengthen their relationship with Jesus Christ.

That week I took an afternoon class on the Psalms. Dr. David Glock, a professor at Emmaus Bible College, took us through the structure and content of several categories of psalms in Scripture. Then he encouraged us to write some of our own.

Before that, my feelings had spilled all over everywhere, like a river overflowing. But this class gave me structures and patterns—the riverbanks to help me channel my thoughts and feelings in a way the Bible itself sanctioned. So I didn't have to feel guilty about those emotions.

Sitting on my camp bunk, tears meandering down my cheeks, I slipped my own words into a common pattern of what's called a "lament" psalm (see the pattern at the end of this devotion). Finally, I could process my emotions with honesty. As I started writing, thoughts and feelings disentangled themselves—as Charles Swindoll puts it.

What a new level of intimacy with my all-knowing God of unfailing love! (See my resulting lament psalm, "Magnified Grief," at the end of this devotion.) But first, I had to be totally honest and vulnerable before Him.

King David knew what it was like to be *overwhelmed* with emotion. He captured his feelings in writing and asked God to listen and answer. So can we. We can pray,

> Oh, Loving Lord, You created us
> with a full range of emotions.
> You know them all anyway
> So please help us
> to talk them over with You
> and find release.

Journal Prompts

We'll look at several categories and patterns of psalms throughout this book—psalms of lament (see below), praise, creation, confession, confidence, wisdom, and more. (All the patterns are also given in the appendix.)

When have you felt extreme grief or pain? Are you going through a difficult season now? Write about it in as much or as little detail as you'd like. Later you'll have an opportunity to write a lament psalm of your own, using the lament patterns (below) as riverbanks for your emotions. My contemporary psalm of this type, "Magnified Grief," follows as an example. Look at the lament patterns below and see if you can recognize its elements in that contemporary psalm.

When you're writing your lament, don't feel obligated to write as formally as I have written in that example. Write honestly from your heart.

Two styles of lament psalm patterns

Help!
Enough!
I trust You
I choose to praise You

Or, more specifically:
Please listen to me, God.
I can't take any more of this.
    Here's how I'm feeling.
    I'm letting it all spill out.
I need You, Lord.
I still believe You care
no matter how bad
the situation may seem right now.

Magnified Grief

A lament psalm
written after the death of friend and brother-in-law
Bob Williams (Willie)

Oh, Lord, my Lord, I cannot understand Your ways.
Your acts often defy my comprehension.
Why do You take the righteous to an early grave
and let the wicked leave more in their wake?
Tears still fill our eyes unbidden—
Do You not see them?
Pain still rends our heart unmended—
Will You not heal it?
To feel the ache ourselves is only doubled
as we watch those closer hurt the more.
With all that heaven holds,
could You not have spared us this grief?
Lord, help me believe that what I can't understand
comes from the same wise hand
that has led me before.
My heart sings, my God,
of Your unfailing love
every waking moment.
Your song fills my mind
as I drift into sleep
every single night.
—Joyce K. Ellis

Author Chris Tiegreen imagines God speaking words like these to us:
"If you remember where we have been together, you'll be much better prepared to trust Me for where we are going together ... I have created you, loved you, been patient with you, redeemed you from your captivity, listened to your prayers and answered them, provided for you, healed you, restored you, and so much more."[4]

2

REMEMBER TO REMEMBER

*My soul will feast and be satisfied,
and I will sing glad songs of praise to you.
As I lie in bed, I remember you ...
because you have always been my help.
In the shadow of your wings I sing for joy.*
—Psalm 63:5–7 (GNT)

Years ago, I read *The Emancipation of Robert Sadler*, the incomprehensible story of a man who lived in slavery on a plantation well into the twentieth century. I'll never forget the image he painted of the red-hot poker his master seared into his flesh. And I still marvel at the supernatural strength the Lord gave Sadler to endure.

It wasn't easy for him to write that book, even with the help of a veteran author. Sadler had blocked out those painful memories for many years. He knew he wasn't the only one who had gone through this ordeal.

"I tried to think back as far as I could remember," he said, "think on things I had long ago buried, and let stay buried." So he prayed this prayer: "Help me to remember it, Lord, so I can tell it just the way it was."[5] Sadler needed to remember in order to forget.

For you and me, sorting through both pleasant and painful memories—especially if journaling about them or creating a psalm from them—can strengthen our faith. The Scriptures overflow with the rally cry of "Remember the Red Sea," so to speak—somewhat like the old battle cry, "Remember the Alamo."

The writers of Scripture seemed to say to the Israelites, "Don't forget the astounding miracle God did by parting the Red Sea for you. (See Exodus 14.) We escaped while our cruel captors, Pharaoh and his Egyptian army, drowned in hot pursuit. If God can do *that*, we can trust Him with anything!"

I have often come to a screeching halt with what I call my Red Sea moments: miscarriage, surgeries, concussion, severe financial crisis, fear-inducing emergencies with our children, and that awful sense that the Enemy was breathing down my neck. As God brings each of us through our own Red Sea moments, our relationship with Him grows, and our intimacy with Him deepens.

But that intimacy only comes when we are honest with Him about how we feel instead of trying to experience the joy before fully dealing with the pain.

Chris Tiegreen writes about the way Jesus comes to His followers in our storms at sea: "[Jesus] reminds us that faith is the key to overcoming, that fear undermines faith, and that keeping our focus on Him destroys fear and builds faith. He teaches and strengthens us best not when the weather is calm but when the waves are about to overwhelm us."[6]

Feeling overwhelmed? What a legacy of honest, unpretentious faith we can leave behind if we'll allow ourselves to be vulnerable before God, and before others, about the waves crashing around us. In contrast, how *unkind* we are when we allow others to feel they're the only ones struggling in the storm. So we can pray,

> Oh, Almighty God, every Red Sea moment
> can demonstrate Your power.
> So please help us to be honest with You
> about everything we're thinking and feeling.
> And remind us of the many Red Seas
> You've brought us through before.
> Praise You, Father!

Journal Prompts

Ask God to help you to be honest with Him about your feelings and desires. Ask Him to help you remember things in your past that you may have buried but need to deal with as you deepen your relationship with Him. In one of Moses' contributions to the Psalms, he writes, *You spread out our sins before you—our secret sins—and you see them all* (Psalm 90:8). So why do we find it so hard to open up to Him?

Capturing memories of *your* past Red Sea moments can encourage you to persevere in future tough times. Following a psalm pattern can help. Seldom can we sit down and pour out all our emotions and compose a psalm at one sitting. So make notes here—or, on the go, in a small notebook or your phone. Jot down feelings, descriptions, names of people and items you're thankful for, changes in your thought patterns, and other ideas.

Write at least one sentence, finishing the words below (from Psalm 42:4) about one of your Red Sea moments. You might note what you're learning: My heart is breaking as I remember _____

OUR HEART PSALMS

OUR HEART PSALMS

In You We Put Our Trust
A praise psalm (excerpts)

Lord, You are our fortress and our strength;
    You are our rock and our salvation.
In You we put our trust,
    for Your righteousness is our hope,
    and Your faithfulness is our sure foundation.

You, O Lord, established the heavens and the earth;
    You appointed the mountains to rise;
    and the seas to sink.
With a word, You called the earth into being;
    with Your breath, You caused the heavens
        to encase Your handiwork.
Stars shimmer in the darkness;
    the moon glistens in the stillness of the night;
    the sun pours forth its brilliance
    —all together they show forth
        Your eternal power and glory
Waters gush forth from springs;
    rivers rush toward the seas;
    oceans pound the shores
    —they, too, shout Your praises.
The hills exclaim Your splendor;
    the trees wear Your wondrous glory
    in their verdant green or golden leaves.
The valley sings a melody of praise,
    as its brooks and ponds reflect Your grace.

Their voices endure
>from generation to generation ....

Lord, You are our fortress and our strength;
You are our rock and our salvation.
In You we put our trust,
for Your righteousness is our hope,
and Your faithfulness is our sure foundation.
—Dr. Ardel B. Caneday
Bible Professor
University of Northwestern St. Paul

As George Matheson (1842–1906) prepared for the ministry, he was going blind. On top of that, the love of his life refused to marry him because she didn't want to be married to a blind man. A few years later, before his sister's wedding, his grief over losing the woman he loved overwhelmed him, and he wrote the following hymn—a psalm of confidence in God, written from a broken heart:[7]

O Love That Wilt Not Let Me Go

O Love that wilt not let me go,
I rest my weary soul in Thee:
I give Thee back the life I owe,
That in Thine ocean depths its flow
may richer, fuller be …
O Joy that seekest me through pain,
I cannot close my heart to thee;
I trace the rainbow through the rain,
And feel the promise is not vain,
That morn shall tearless be.
—George Matheson
Scottish hymn writer

Prayer ... is the means by which our language becomes honest, true, and personal in response to God ... We get everything in our lives out in the open before God ... The Psalms ... are earthy and rough. They are not genteel. They are not the prayers of nice people, couched in cultural language.[8]
—Eugene H. Peterson

3

RELEASE THE PRESSURE VALVE

You have changed my sadness into a joyful dance; you have taken away my sorrow and surrounded me with joy. So I will not be silent; I will sing praise to you. LORD, YOU ARE MY GOD; I will give you thanks forever.
—Psalm 30:11–12 (GNT)

In the middle of a Minnesota winter (both of climate and soul), my husband and I escaped briefly from a weariness that had threatened to drown me for more than two years.

My parents, in failing health, needed to move immediately from their apartment to a healthcare facility. So my sister and I had thirty days to clean and empty their apartment: a big task when my Depression-era dad (who, by that point, had Alzheimer's) couldn't throw anything away. In fact, my mom, in a wheelchair, used to cram "throwables" into black trash bags when he was out of the apartment and wheel herself (with garbage bags on her lap) to dispose of the trash in the chute at the end of the hall. Otherwise, Dad would surely "rescue" something they might need one day.

The big task loomed larger because we discovered—in a box of paid bills, decades old—some uncashed savings bonds. So we had to sort through every piece of paper before throwing anything away. It seemed I was even shredding nonessential documents in my sleep! I often worked at my parents' apartment from early morning to eleven at night or later—with my sister and husband helping when they weren't at work.

Then came the endless, infuriating paperwork and phone calls to comply with all the government assistance requirements.

But when responsibilities eased for a bit, Steve and I headed for Florida. As I sat on a white-sugary beach—my emotions as turbulent as the waves—my heart welled up with praise and gratitude for all the Lord had brought us through by His grace.

In the Psalms class I had taken at camp, I learned to write not only lament psalms but also *praise* psalms—particularly *creation* psalms. These proclaimed my trust in my Creator God who sees and understands and has everything under control—

whether *I* feel in control or not. (See the resulting creation psalm, "Eager Praise," at the end of this devotion.)

When the overwhelming weighs heavy on us, we're not always able to escape to another location, but we can look for (or create) quiet moments to refocus—*keeping our eyes on Jesus, the champion who initiates and perfects our faith* (Hebrews 12:2).

I had been dwelling too much on how difficult things had been. But when I focused, instead, on the beauty of God's creation, it was like releasing a pressure valve.

Of course, we can write praise psalms anytime—not just when we need stress relief. Here's a brief example:

> Will anyone praise the Lord with me today?
> Oh, gracious Father, we owe every breath to You.
> Every time we breathe in,
> it's an opportunity to remember Your faithfulness.
> Every time we breathe out,
> it's an opportunity to praise You for Your goodness.
> May we never take You—
> or the breath You give us—
> for granted.
> All praise to our Giver of Life!
> —Joyce K. Ellis

You may be going through an intensely emotional time (of joy or pain) right now. Or you may need to work through some hurts and painful memories of the past. As you read the pages ahead, abandon your defenses, and allow yourself to write freely. God longs for us to be open, honest, and vulnerable. In response, He allows us the privilege of a deeper, more intimate relationship with Him. So we can pray,

> Oh, God of Creation,
> to gaze upon the beauty, immensity,
> and variety of Your handiwork
> brings comfort and perspective.
> So please help us make time
> to enjoy all You have made
> as we focus on Your Greatness.

Journal Prompts

My prayer is that these thoughts will inspire you to join me, digging into the Psalms and finding a voice, a structure, and a channel for expressing your most honest feelings to God. He knows each one anyway and loves us all the more.

Writing a praise psalm doesn't have to be complicated. Some of the simplest praise psalms contain two, sometimes three, main parts. Notice how the psalm "Eager Praise" (below) uses these elements:

Introduction or call to praise:
> Examples
>> Great is the Lord, and most worthy of praise
>> Come praise the Lord with me
>> Hallelujah
>> Praise the Lord

Body: Here's why—reasons to praise, usually beginning with the words *for* or *because*

Restatement of call to praise or further words of praise (optional)

_____
_____
_____
_____
_____
_____
_____
_____
_____
_____
_____
_____
_____
_____
_____

Eager Praise
A creation psalm

My Creator-King,
how awesome You are above all creation.
The whole earth owes You infinite praise.
The ocean waves scramble up the beach,
racing each other to praise You.
As constant as the surf tumbling over the sand
is the love You lavish upon us.
As numerous as the shells creeping ashore
are the children You've created.
Yet You see the unique beauty of each one in infinite variety,
and each one shouts your ingenious design.
My Creator-King,
how awesomely Your creation sings Your praise.
—Joyce K. Ellis

To study [the Psalms] is to make a strange journey of ups and downs, falling and rising, despair and exaltation.[9]
—Dietrich Bonhoeffer

4

NAVIGATE THE SWELLS OF EMOTION

*I cry out to God Most High,
to God who will fulfill his purpose for me.*
—Psalm 57:2

My husband and I don't often get a winter vacation, but one time, we boarded a boat at John's Pass, south of Clearwater, Florida, for a new adventure: deep-sea fishing. As inexperienced anglers, we didn't know what to expect.

When we learned how many passengers would be on the boat, I envisioned ninety fisherpersons, casting their lines, shoulder to shoulder, on the narrow passageway surrounding the boat. I was terrified we'd be embedding fishhooks in each other's scalps and earlobes—giving a whole new meaning to the term *body piercing*.

About ten miles from shore, the crew gave us quick pointers and some squid chunks for bait.

The crew then showed us how to drop the line and sinker into the raucous waves and let the fish on the ocean's floor discover their lunch.

My emotions somersaulted through cycles: Delight at the slight tug on the thirty-foot line. Fear at finding no land in sight. Excitement at seeing my first fish swaying in the stiff winds. Disappointment at saying goodbye to the many that got away. Joy at watching Steve "reel in" a yellow and brown polka-dotted blowfish. Amusement at seeing our guide blow up one of those potentially poisonous fish like a balloon and serving it, volleyball style, back into the ocean. Jealousy at hearing how many more fish the people were catching on the other side of the boat.

When the crew navigated to another area, Steve and I stumbled inside. Trying to correlate our steps with the rolling waves proved challenging—up and down, down and up. After a while, we learned the rhythm of the dance—grasping anything in sight for support.

My life has been a lot like that: the up-down, down-up rolling waves of emotion that have sent me scrambling for anything solid to hang on to. That's why I love the psalms of Scripture.

Within a few verses or pages, we can
- laugh with joy

- weep in pain (physical or emotional)
- ask why without fearing reprisal
- take courage in our God who has delivered us before
- feel terror over loved ones running away or attacking
- cheer about fresh victories
- grieve over our ugly words (or thoughts or actions)
- and charge ahead with bold trust when we can't distinguish the *boundaries* of the tunnel much less the light at the end of it.

God moved people like you and me—from humble servants to world influencers—to communicate their honest, intimate feelings to Almighty God. Their psalms generally fall into two main categories: *praises* and *laments*.

Praises are like flower bouquets of appreciation.
Laments are like overstuffing the suggestion box with complaints.
Praises are like songs in a major key.
Laments are like songs in a minor key.

But even the laments (most of them) sound a chord of confidence in God at the end. The people writing them admonish themselves to praise the Lord in the midst of the crisis. They encourage other believers to join in, praising Him.

Why? Because they know He always does what is right (even if we don't understand it). And if God is the One we turn to in our difficulty, distress, or disillusionment, doesn't that also bring Him praise?

The psalms of Scripture model ways to find our own voice—baring every emotion, thought, word, action, and event of our lives before Him. In exchange, we receive His intimate, loving embrace and a renewed perspective on what we're going through. So we can pray,

> Oh, God of Peace, our emotions can rise
> and tumble quickly.
> So please help us find Your equilibrium
> by honestly baring our heart—
> hiding nothing,
> pretending nothing,
> confiding everything
> in You.

Journal Prompts

Note at least one event in which you soared with the heights of joy and one event in which you crashed into the depths of pain or sorrow. Confide in God. Write your honest emotions about one of those times in as much or little detail as you wish. Pray for transparency and for His equilibrium. Begin (or continue) to write a psalm about what you're feeling and learning.

OUR HEART PSALMS

Mood Swings

Some people might accuse the Psalms of being bipolar or manic-depressive—swinging like a pendulum from ecstatic highs to suicidal lows. King David wrote this:

> *I will exalt you, my God and King ...*
> *I will praise you every day ...*
> *Great is the Lord! He is most worthy of praise!*
> *No one can measure his greatness.*
> —Psalm 145:1–3

Yet that same man, "a man after God's own heart" (perhaps partly because he wrote honestly from his own heart), also penned this:

> *How long must I struggle with*
> *anguish in my soul,*
> *with sorrow in my heart every day?...*
> *Turn and answer me, O Lord my God!*
> *Restore the sparkle to my eyes, or I will die.*
> —Psalm 13:2–3

Scripture's psalms deal with life as it is, not what we'd like it to be. God created us with emotions as well as minds and bodies, spirits and souls. And He walks with us in our feelings as well as every other aspect of life.

II

FEELINGS

Section Note

When people recommend that we begin prayers with praise, they often cite the Lord's Prayer as an example: Jesus began His model prayer by praising (hallowing) God's name.

That's a great place to start. But, as I said before, sometimes frustration gnawed at me when I used that pattern. I felt dishonest trying to drum up praise when my heart wanted to cry out in pain, anger, or confusion. Was I trying to butter up God so He'd listen when I finally told Him how I felt?

If we use Jesus' prayers as examples, remember His prayer on the cross. In three torturous hours, He suffered an eternity's worth of punishment for your sins and mine—past, present, and future. In infinite agony, He didn't feel obligated to shower God with praises. He blurted out His true feelings in what may be the most excruciating lament ever prayed: *"My God, My God, why have You forsaken Me?"* (Matthew 27:46 HCSB).

In the blackest hole of history, our precious Savior screamed out His pain, holding nothing back. His prayer exemplifies the most honest, intimate outpouring of emotions before our Father.

Yes, God allows us to "start where we are."

Although this section begins with happy feelings, feel free to skip around in your reading to navigate whatever emotions you're experiencing at the time. You can use the patterns given as riverbanks for expressing your heart psalms to God.

Trust in the Lord and do good ... Take delight in the Lord, and he will give you your heart's desires. Commit everything you do to the Lord. Trust him, and he will help you.
—Psalm 37:3–5

The happiness which brings enduring worth to life is not the superficial happiness that is dependent on circumstances. It is the happiness and contentment that fills the soul even in the midst of the most distressing of circumstances and the most adverse environment.[10]

—Billy Graham

5

FEELING HAPPY

*Make me walk along the path
of your commands,
for that is where my happiness is found.*
—Psalm 119:35

Having married at the age of nineteen and given birth to my first child a couple of months before I turned twenty-one, I pressed the pause button on my college plans. I wasn't sure I'd ever realize that dream. But years later, when our firstborn enrolled in college, Steve and I discovered our son would qualify for more financial aid if more than one family member attended college at the same time. I jumped at the opportunity.

Starting college at the age of thirty-nine is probably the hardest thing I've ever done. With a middle-schooler and two teenagers of our own at home—and a teenage friend of our daughter's living with us—everything became more challenging. But after squeezing four years of studies into five, I became the first of my family to graduate from college.

My college graduation day, my wedding day, and the days I gave birth to our three babies (now grown), have been the happiest days in my life so far (not necessarily in that order).

Happiness can come from a friendship begun, a goal achieved, a crisis resolved, a purpose found, a dream realized, an illness healed. Happiness can come from a new love, a fresh insight, an answered prayer, an infusion of hope.

Happiness can bubble up quickly but evaporate just as fast. The exhilaration of a high exam score can be dashed when the professor announces she inadvertently attributed the brainiac's score to you and your pitiful results to Señor Brainiac. The excitement of a promotion can crash when next week's downsizing move results in massive layoffs. The ecstasy of receiving a normal MRI can shatter when other labs tell a different story.

Happiness is a conscious choice. An attitude. We can *choose* to be happy *in God* even when it would be unnatural to be happy about our situation. In fact, that's often when we become more intimate with Him. And we can be sure that He filters everything we experience through His loving fingers.

Our Enemy, Satan, throws a lot at us—feelings of failure, scary circumstances, lies, accusations—all designed to derail our faith. But God's love screens everything before it gets to us: *God keeps his promise, and he will not allow you to be tested beyond your power to remain firm; at the time you are put to the test, he will give you the strength to endure it, and so provide you with a way out* (1 Corinthians 10:13 GNT).

Happiness, like joy, is worth sharing. Doesn't your heart beat faster when you hear a friend's excited voice on the phone, saying, "I just had to call to tell you the good news"? Maybe that's the delight God feels when we share our happiness with Him.

The apostle James wrote, "Are any of you happy? You should sing praises" (5:13). So why not write psalms of happiness? Our gratitude-turned-thanksgiving tickles the heart of God. He *needs* nothing yet smiles when we offer our puny praise anyway.

As I write this, we have recently celebrated Thanksgiving Day in the USA. Although, for some people, the day often disintegrates into food, football, and a footrace to beat the Black-Friday-Eve rush, believers in Jesus Christ have many reasons to be happy and thankful. So we can pray,

Oh, precious Eternal God of no limits,
You've given us so much,
You've spared us so much,
You've demonstrated Your love for us so much—
every moment of every day.
So please help us remember to thank You so much!

Journal Prompts

What can you be happy about today? What might you have taken for granted lately?

Happiness shines brighter following a resolved crisis. Whenever we're feeling happy, it can be a great time to write a thanksgiving psalm—whether it's Thanksgiving season or not.

Jot some notes below. And, if you'd like, start writing a thanksgiving psalm, using the riverbanks (pattern) below. Note the way a thanksgiving psalm can contrast—and can build on—a lament psalm:

Lament psalm may say	Thanksgiving psalm may say
	Praise the Lord
Help!	I cried out for help
Enough!	This is how bad it was
I trust You	I trusted You; You did it
I choose to praise You	I promised to praise You, so I praise You now

Otherwise, simply follow the pattern in the previous chapter for a psalm that gives thanks to God for whatever has ticked up your happiness meter today.

Let the morrow be what it may, our God is the God of tomorrow. Whatever events may have happened, which to us are unknown, our Jehovah is God of the unknown as well as of the known. We are determined to trust the Lord, come what may. If the very worst should happen, our God is still the greatest and best. Therefore will we not fear.[11]
—Charles Spurgeon

Are you feeding your fears or fueling your faith?[12]
—Luci Shaw

6

FEELING FEARFUL

*My heart pounds in my chest ...
Fear and trembling overwhelm me, and
I can't stop shaking.*
—Psalm 55:4–5

When a single friend invited me to join her for a beach vacation, she didn't have to twist my arm. Two middle-aged colleagues, both desperate for a break from work deadlines and home responsibilities. Unhurried time. Reading. Staring at the ocean waves rolling in. What a wonderful few days of relaxation!

One morning a bright yellow parachute—with a huge, black smiley face—floated through the air, high above the surf. An indistinguishable someone dangled from the parachute, tethered to a yacht far below.

"I wish I weren't so afraid of heights," I told my friend. "That parasailing looks like so much fun. But I could never summon the courage to do it."

The next day, she informed me that she had booked a parasailing trip for us, and she would not let me back out. We would sail in tandem, she assured me, so I wouldn't be alone. It would be fun!

My friend, a woman who has yet to find a roller coaster she doesn't love, couldn't feel the burning in the pit of my stomach. She hadn't been with me when I froze, years before, trying to cross a high railroad bridge without handrails. She didn't see me crawling on my hands and knees on that bridge, retreating to safety.

I knew I had to conquer this fear. It symbolized so many others in my life—fear of failure, fear of the unknown, fear to take risks in my career, fears regarding my children, and more.

Sometimes overcoming physical challenges and fears helps us overcome mental, emotional, and spiritual ones—and vice versa. It's another Red-Sea-moment issue (see chapter 2). Fearful times can help us stretch our faith muscles, but I was letting fear rob me of an exciting adventure.

That night, as I tried to fall asleep, I remembered a bedtime conversation I'd had with my seven-year-old granddaughter one evening before praying with her. She slept in a downstairs bedroom and had a fear of the dark. So I taught her this Bible verse: *When I am afraid, I will put my trust in you [God]* (Psalm 56:3). She relaxed a bit when I reminded her that, in the darkness, God watched over her the same way He did in the daylight.

As I wrestled with the parasailing issue, I reminded myself that God would be with me in the air the same way He's with me on the ground. I could trust Him.

Not long before that trip, I read what has become one of my all-time favorite books, *The Crime of Living Cautiously*. I reread it often, and my copy is full of underlining and highlighting. Sticky-note flags fly from the margins of numerous pages.

In that book, author Luci Shaw gives this pointed pep talk: "Feel the fear and do it anyway ... Shoulder aside the fear, as you would a curtain in a doorway as you pass through."[13]

I can't avoid everything that makes me afraid. But I can trust in God's strength, shoulder the fear aside, and move on.

My friend gave me another parasailing incentive. She knows I will go to great *lengths* to snap an amazing photo. How about great *heights*? She helped me imagine the amazing pictures I could get while floating through the brilliant blue sky over the ocean.

So I bought a waterproof disposable camera and, with a pounding heart, boarded the boat and allowed myself to be trapped in a harness below my friend.

I couldn't believe how gently we rose above the water. Excitement and adrenalin all but replaced fear in the freedom of letting go. What a reward I would have missed if I hadn't followed Luci Shaw's advice: "Feel the fear and do it anyway"!

During another fearful time, I was reading through *The One-Year-Bible*™ each day. Before long, I realized that at least once in each week's readings (from Old and New Testaments), God whispered or shouted precious fear-slaying assurances to me:
"Fear not."
"Don't be afraid."
"I am with you."

So we can pray,
Oh, Fear-Slaying God,
so many things in our world,
in our jobs,
and in our hearts
foster fear.
So please help us to acknowledge our fears,

draw on Your strength and peace,
and move ahead to do what You're showing us to do.

Journal Prompts

1. Note below one or more fears that plague you. In what areas has God helped you find a measure of peace? Mention any ways He has helped you (or is helping you) shoulder those fears aside. What verses of Scripture help you trust Him? When you're ready, be honest with God about your fears and write an appropriate psalm, such as one of these types:
   - confession psalm—acknowledge a lack of trusting God
   - thanksgiving psalm—thank God for helping you through a fearful situation
   - praise psalm—praise God for being a God who cares about our fears.

   (See the appendix for a list of patterns or elements you can include.)

2. While reading Scripture's Psalms, pay attention to the psalmists' honest acknowledgment of their fears and God's repeated commands, "Don't be afraid. Trust me."

3. Think about Luci Shaw's question at the beginning of this devotion. In what ways are you "feeding your fears or fueling your faith"?

Fear Paradox

Life can be scary, Lord.
I confess I feel fear.
I fear uncertainty.
I know that fear is a natural emotion—
even a healthy method of self-preservation.
But I know some of my fears are unhealthy,
irrational, joy-robbing.
They can be self-destruct messages from the Enemy.
They can keep me from obeying You.
I don't know how You're going to solve
this present fearful situation.
To pretend I'm not afraid would be a lie.
But You've talked me off scary cliffs like this before,
reminding me that Your power and presence
are stronger than my fear.
I have a choice:
let fear paralyze me
or let You show me what You can do.
I lay down my defenses
and choose to trust You.
—Joyce K. Ellis

Life in the pit stinks. Yet for all its rottenness doesn't the pit do this much? It forces you to look upward. Someone from up there must come down here and give you a hand.[14]

—Max Lucado

7

FEELING DEPRESSED

Why am I so depressed?
Why this turmoil within me?
Put your hope in God, for
I will still praise Him,
my Savior and my God.
—Psalm 42:5 (HCSB)

My three preschoolers fighting for my attention. My own mother blocking out the sun with drapes drawn, needing my frequent help with her housework. My dashed expectations regarding life goals. My propensity to take on more responsibilities than doable. Why would I be depressed?

When I dared to tell Christian friends I felt I was spiraling downward, I heard comments like these: "You shouldn't be depressed." "Aren't you trusting the Lord enough?" "Everybody gets down now and then. You'll be okay."

So I lived far too long in the land of incomprehensible, inexpressible, inconsolable emotions. I've often described my depression as feeling like I was living at the bottom of a deep, dark well.

Little by little, over the years, the Lord has helped me grow through these Red Sea moments. But I still, sometimes, feel depression sucking at my heels. I cry out to God, "Please hang on to me. I don't want to go back there again."

Sometimes when people ask me what's wrong, I handle it with humor—something like "There's nothing wrong with me that a month in Bermuda wouldn't cure." But, to be honest, I've often wished I could run away, escape our messed-up world and my own personal failures. Depression, whether a low-grade temperature or a raging fever, can debilitate us. And in those times, we need the Great Physician's prescription of hope.

Many of the psalm writers of Scripture knew depression. In fact, the verse at the beginning of this devotion (Psalm 42:5) is repeated, verbatim, twice more: Psalm 42:11 and Psalm 43:5.

But the more I'm reading the Psalms, the more I see how often the psalm writers start where they are in their emotions—a place of pain, confusion, frustration, depression. Then they come to a huge turning point, where they regain their emotional equilibrium in God. Sometimes that turning point, a spiritual hinge that changes their perspective, appears quickly. Other times, the writers go on and on, pouring out their misery before they put their hope in God instead of dwelling on the pain.

Many years ago, my friend and choir director Terry White delighted in pointing out obscure (to me) musical terms. One that stuck in my mind—primarily because he seemed so fond of it—is a Picardy third. When a piece of music has been in a minor (sad-sounding) key and then strikes a major (happy-sounding) chord at the end, that switch is called a Picardy third.

I couldn't help but think of that musical term as I noticed the abrupt turning point in many lament psalms. After detailing painful situations, psalm writers often do an about-face and praise God or affirm trust in Him.

That's the Picardy third—the major chord of hope in whatever minor chords of life we're facing. Instead of complaining to others, we can let our emotions slosh out and bring them to the One who alone can do anything about the situation. Spiritual and emotional maturity develops as we understand that conflicting emotions can coexist in the grace-filled arms of God.

It may take a while for us to reach that point. But sometimes this kind of pattern helps:

> Lord, this is the bad place I'm in.
> I need Your _____ [name an attribute of God's].
> (Thoughts of that characteristic brings turning point)
> I praise You that You are _____
> and that I have seen You _____.

We may have to scribble down a lot of anger and pain before the Lord can bring healing. But during the process, we can look for the major chord He wants to strike in our hearts. So we can pray,

> Oh, Changeless Lord,
> Our world breeds discouragement, sadness,
> and depression,
> emotions that can sidetrack us from doing
> what You've called us to do.
> So please help us dump out
> all the negative feelings before You
> So we can fill our hearts
> with Your perspective and hope.

Come quickly, Lord, and answer me,
for my depression deepens.
Don't turn away from me,
or I will die.
—Psalm 143:7

Journal Prompts

Jot down a few notes about one or more times you've felt sorrow, grief, despair, depression, or similar emotions. Start writing a lament psalm about one of these times, using this pattern:

> Help!
> Enough!
> I trust You.
> I choose to praise You

See the lament psalm example below, written after my mother had a stroke at age fifty-five—a time when I struggled with sadness and depression. Where do you see the elements of the lament pattern? Where is the turning point?

_____

_____

_____

_____

_____

Disequilibrium
A lament psalm

Oh, Lord, why? It's so hard for me to take it.
She's faced health hurdles before, but this?
I didn't know it could hurt me so.
A mother is someone strong …
someone who can read a story to your children,
or play a game to entertain them.
But what about when speech is incoherent, logic askew,
simple game rules complicated?
When I'm impatient, forgive me …
You, precious Lord, are sovereign.
You store our questions' answers in a bottle
that only You can see through.
I choose to trust Your loving hand—
invisible though it may be—
and praise You that Your grace
doesn't depend on me.[15]
—Joyce K. Ellis

Today
A lament psalm

Is there no end to the pain, Lord?
Pain of heart. Pain of body. Pain of mind.
Must I really accept
That this is my new normal?
Are You still here, Lord?
Can You hear me? Right now I can't tell.
Some days I feel like giving up.
I long for Home.
But You keep reminding me
of all the times You've brought me
through in the past
and that You, alone,
will perfectly time my departure.
So I trust You for this "today,"
and the next
and the next.
Help me to be and do what I can today
by Your grace.
And I will trust You for another "today"
tomorrow.
—Joyce K. Ellis

Norway Travels
A creation psalm

Come, praise the Lord with me
for visions of His life-giving touch.
Around each bend in the road
something new to take our breath away, Father.
How I praise You for
glacier-fed waterfalls gushing
or trickling or meandering—
roaring or whispering,
from heaven to earth,
images of "every good gift comes from above."
Praise the Lord for His life-giving touch.
—Joyce K. Ellis

Happy the soul that has been awed by a view of God's majesty.[16]
—Arthur W. Pink

8

FEELING AWED BY GOD'S CREATION

*O Lord, our Lord, your majestic name
fills the earth!
Your glory is higher than the heavens ...
When I look at the night sky and
see the work of your fingers—
the moon and the stars you set in place—
what are mere mortals that you
should think about them,
human beings that you should care
for them?*
—Psalm 8:1, 3–4

I love those stop-in-your-tracks moments God gives us: a stunning fuchsia sunset, a delicate lavender rose, a stark-white moon reflecting off the mirror of a dark, tranquil lake. Often we respond spontaneously, "That's beautiful, Lord!" or "Praise You, Father!"

Many years ago, rainbows became powerful reminders to me that God still keeps His promises—even as He has kept His promise to Noah never again to destroy the whole earth with water.

Every now and then it seems as though the Lord sticks a rainbow in the sky like a giant, decorative sticky note to remind me of His promise never to leave me—never to leave any of His followers—no matter how dark the storm clouds are.

So, in our family we don't take rainbows lightly.

One stormy summer afternoon our daughter, son-in-law, and grandchildren (then ages three and one), came over for dinner. While we were eating in the kitchen, I looked out the window and noticed the sun—low in the sky—had broken through the clouds in the west while the eastern sky remained threatening.

"Looks like the weather's ripe for a rainbow," I said. Running outside, barefoot in the rain, I peered around the side of the house, and, sure enough, a brilliant arc of colors lit up the sky. Returning for our grandkids, I rushed them out to see God's colorful spectacle and told them about Noah and promises and our faithful God. And they caught my excitement.

David wrote: *Let each generation tell its children of your mighty acts; let them proclaim your power* (Psalm 145:4). And he wrote down psalms of praise to pass along to generation after generation after generation—for centuries.

Although it's difficult to know for sure the circumstances surrounding each of David's psalms, I imagine he may have been strolling in the palace courtyard one balmy, cloudless evening. And perhaps the king, thrilling at God's artwork on the dark canvas spread out above, sat down and, by the light of a full moon, expressed his feelings about his Creator. Maybe these words became the Scripture quoted at the beginning of this devotion.

Read that passage again. Those are words of awe! Everywhere we look, reasons to praise Him abound. But sometimes we get too busy to look. And to respond.

Yet if *we* don't praise Him, God says that even dirty, lifeless old rocks *will*. (See Luke 19:37–40.)

While traveling through the Wisconsin countryside, Steve and I came around a bend and spotted what I suppose was the handiwork of someone with a sense of humor and vision, someone who knew that passage in Luke 19.

There, embedded in the side of the hill, dozens of big, whitewashed rocks spelled out the words, *Praise the Lord.* I laughed and hoped *my* praise would never be deficient enough that the rocks have to muster some type of voice for praise. So we can pray,

> Oh, All-powerful Creator,
> sometimes I suffer from praise deficiency.
> I simply must not be paying attention.
> Please wake me up to all the truly awesome
> sights, sounds, textures, tastes, and fragrances
> You have surrounded me with in Your creation.
> I don't want to hear any rocks singing.

Journal Prompts

Where is your favorite getaway place to enjoy God's creation? What location near your home might spark ideas for a creation psalm? Pay attention to all five of your God-given senses today. What elements of nature inspire you to praise God? Avoid clichés as you jot down ideas for a creation psalm. Here's a simple creation psalm pattern from Scripture to help you start writing one:

Creation psalms (patterned after Psalm 8)

direct address to God
general statement of praise (front bookend)
God's supremacy and greatness
specific illustrations from nature
contrast of human frailty
gift of dignity God bestows on us
human supremacy over the rest of creation
identical statement of praise (as v. 1)
direct address to God
generalized praise statement (back bookend)

Write freely and honestly.

What a Morning!

A creation psalm (excerpts)

My Lord, what a morning!
Lord, You have created so much beauty around me.
I struggle even to name it for fear of subtracting from it.
What genius! ... Where do you get Your ideas? ...
How did You think of green?
And where did the smoothness of cream come from? ...
Words are so confining ...
I cannot contain all that You are ...
Thank You and thank You and thank You.
My Lord, what a morning!
—Linnea Fellows

JOYCE K. ELLIS

Unending Praise
A creation psalm

Almighty Creator,
You are worthy of endless praise
from everything You have created.
How I love to observe and praise You
for all You have made!
You have filled this world
with exquisite artistic works.
You have hung up galaxies of stars and planets
as if they were chandeliers,
shining out praises to You.
You have created an ocean gallery of coral sculptures,
fish choreography and whales singing—all for You.
You have trimmed the jungles,
forests, and towns
with Your creations excited
to bring glory to You.
The leaves on the trees clap to bring You praise.
Rabbits hop to bring You praise.
Squirrels scurry to bring You praise.
Deer glide through the trees
to bring You praise.
Peacocks show off Your feather painting
to bring You praise.
It's like creation doesn't ever want the praise to end.
I can't help but join in, Almighty Creator.
You are worthy of endless praise.
—Joyce K. Ellis

Note
Scripture often uses the phrase *fear of God*, ironically, to describe the trust relationship we have with Him—a reverential awe. An intimate distance.
- We come to know Him more and more intimately the longer we walk with Him.
- He draws us nearer and nearer to His heart.
- There's still a distance or gap we can never span completely because of His absolute holiness.
- He is God and we will never be.
- Still, the more intimately acquainted with Him we become, the more we can celebrate Him in praise.

Hymn psalms spring from that deepening intimacy. Note this contrast:
- Thanksgiving psalms direct our praise to God for His deeds (relating what He has done for us).
- Hymn psalms direct our praise to God for His character (describing who He is). That's why scholars often refer to hymn psalms as *descriptive praise*.

We overflow with thanksgiving when God's mercies and blessings fill us up. The amount of favor being poured into us is greater than the capacity of our hearts. When we realize the size of God's generosity, we can't help but be grateful.[17]
—Chris Tiegreen

9

FEELING GRATEFUL FOR WHO GOD IS

I will praise you, Lord, with all my heart ...
I will be filled with joy because of you.
—Psalm 9:1–2

A few years ago, Steve and I sold our house in order to move back to the area where we raised our family. But house hunting bordered on the frantic as the day approached when we had to turn over the keys of our former home to the new owners. We still hadn't found a house, and I didn't like the option of living under a Minnesota bridge, especially in winter.

We prayed. We knew we belonged to the God who goes by the name *Jehovah-Jireh*, God, our Provider. So we prayed some more.

I do not possess apartment-dweller DNA. But a short time before our closing date on the old house, while I was teaching at a conference in Pennsylvania, Steve found an apartment with a month-to-month lease. It could work until we found the just-right place we were trusting Jehovah-Jireh to provide.

But what Steve and I hoped would only be a month or two stretched into eighteen months. The apartment-dwelling challenge dragged by, made worse by two health crises. But we trusted that God's timing is perfect. And we knew the house our realtor showed us was the right one when we saw the street name—a name that reflected God's provision.

Oh, how grateful my husband and I are for every new discovery of who God is! Yes, I can write in my journal, "Thank You, Lord, that You are my Provider." But how much sweeter if I praise Him in a more specific thanksgiving psalm, which I can re-read later for encouragement. Something like this:

> Praise the Lord, our Jehovah-Jireh!
> Thank You for the many ways You have provided for us
> in the past.
> Sometimes when I lie awake in bed,
> worried about how we're going to pay for
> the expensive car repairs,
> the medical procedure not covered by insurance,
> or the replacement of the most-recent appliance
> to give up the ghost,
> I tell my heart to remember—

> to remember I can trust You
> because we have seen Your hand so many times.
> You've reached out at the just-right time
> to provide finances in unexpected ways.
> You've multiplied my strength
> when I thought I couldn't go on.
> You've brought healing—in Your time
> and given strength to endure what
> You've chosen not to heal.
> I pour out my thanksgiving again and again
> for I know You will never resign as Jehovah-Jireh.
> Help me keep telling our family's stories
> of Your provision,
> and may all who hear them
> praise You along with us!
> Praise the Lord, our Jehovah-Jireh!
> —Joyce K. Ellis

We, as believers, delight God's heart whenever we remind ourselves, and each other, how great He is—in specific ways we have experienced.

David was talking to himself when he wrote, *Let all that I am praise the Lord; may I never forget the good things he does for me* (Psalm 103:2). By the end of that psalm, he asks everyone and everything to join in the praise: the angels, the heavenly hosts, all His servants, everything God has made.

As I often say, I believe our psalms of praise tickle the heart of God. He *needs* nothing, yet He smiles when we offer our totally inadequate gratitude anyway. So we can pray,

> Oh, Ever-faithful Lord,
> I am truly grateful for who You are.
> Your trustworthiness and unfailing love astound me.
> But sometimes I let life's challenges get the upper hand.
> So please help me to nurture a grateful heart.
> Keep opening my eyes, Lord,
> to Your greatness, Your sovereignty, and Your power,
> and may my hard-learned response be one of gratitude.

Journal Prompts

When you think about who God is and how great He is, are there visual images you associate with those ideas? Make note of them here for potential use in a psalm of praise and thanksgiving. What attribute of God touches your heart the most? What Scripture verses declare this about Him? (A search of biblegateway.com can help. Or google "Names of God" or "Attributes of God" for ideas.) How have you experienced this characteristic in your relationship with Him? If you want to write a psalm of thanksgiving about it, avoid clichés and let God hear your own fresh expressions of praise from your experience. Go for it!

A pattern for descriptive praise and thanksgiving psalms

Introduction or call to praise:
> Examples
>> Great is the Lord, and most worthy of praise
>> Come praise the Lord with me
>> Hallelujah
>> Praise the Lord

Body: Here's why—reasons to praise, usually beginning with the words *for* or *because*

Restatement of call to praise or further words of praise (optional)

_____
_____
_____
_____
_____
_____
_____
_____
_____
_____
_____
_____
_____

Adoration
A praise psalm

O Lord, my Lord, how magnificent is Your name!
How incomprehensible is the scope of Your creativity!
When I think about how You flung into space
10 trillion galaxies,
How You designed and launched
8.7 million species of animals,
391,000 species of plants,
10,000 species of birds,
All designed to thrive within the ecosystem
You created for them,
When I meditate on the ingenuity of Your design
for the human body:
Each gland and organ and system
intricately created for our survival,
our enjoyment, our well-being—
with provision for reproduction and a brain
with infinite possibilities—
there are no words adequate to praise Your name!
Most astounding of all, though,
I am but a speck in Your universe,
I am made in Your image,
Unworthily loved by a Creator God,
Sacrificially redeemed by Your Son,
Graciously sealed by Your Holy Spirit.
O Lord, my Lord, how magnificent is Your name!
—Sharon Sheppard

How Many Times?
A thanksgiving psalm

Holy God, my soul begged for mercy.
I wondered how often You could keep forgiving me
for the same sins,
the same failed attempts to do what is right,
the same lack of self-control over and over.
How many times could YOU forgive me?
Seven times?
Seventy times seven?
Do You ever stop forgiving sooner
than Peter thought was generous to forgive others?
No! There is no pardoning God like You!
Jesus' Ultimate Sacrifice paid everything I owe.
I thank You that all that was left for me
was to accept Your restoring love for inside change.
By Your grace I yield to Your control for "next time."
You deserve my love and gratitude forever.
—Joyce K. Ellis

My Rock
A thanksgiving psalm

I will praise You, Lord, and tell of your kindness to me.
I called on You in my despair and pain.
I was completely out of strength and resources of my own.
But Your Word came in power to address my need.
Your promises became a rock to dig my fingers into
as I dangled at the edge of a cliff.
They gave me hope and a reason to believe I wouldn't fall.
You held on to my wrists when I was too tired to cling.
Your arms of love
—expressed through Your saints—
surrounded me and lifted me up to firm ground.
I praise You, my strength and my salvation,
my deliverer and my hope.
—Doreen Stewart

Let us expect that God is going to use us. Let us have courage and go forward, looking to God to do great things.[18]
—Dwight L. Moody

If God is the strength of our heart, no weakness really matters.[19]
—Chris Tiegreen

10

FEELING INSECURE

*A song for pilgrims ascending to Jerusalem.
Those who trust in the Lord are as
secure as Mount Zion;
they will not be defeated but will
endure forever.*
—Psalm 125:1

I stood with more than a dozen Christian journalists at the bottom of the Southern Steps of the temple ruins in Jerusalem. Several of us had an opportunity to present a site-relevant devotion at various places we visited, and it was my turn here.

I led the group in reading one of the psalms among what are called The Songs of Ascent in the book of Psalms. The people of Israel recited these types of psalms during their long pilgrimages to the City of David, even on their way up the temple steps on the way to worship.

We read verse one of the psalm together on the first step, verse two on the second step, progressing upward until we finished the psalm. My heart thrilled as I felt the sure footing of those stone steps, thousands of years old, beneath my feet as we read the verses affirming our faith in our unshakeable God. Jesus and His followers had walked up and down those same steps many times.

Because I hadn't fully recovered from a torn-meniscus surgery, I struggled to keep up with everyone, and, I confess, the trip stretched my faith. I felt insecure and somewhat intimidated by my more experienced colleagues.

Yet there we all stood on equal footing, step by step, on solid rock—secure as Mount Zion itself because we had built our lives on the Lord, our Eternal Rock. He was the One we were trusting for our salvation. What an exhilarating thought! What security!

Insecurities come in all shapes and sizes—from finances to friendships to physical appearance—and more. But chief among them can be uncertainty about what will happen when we die. When I was a child, I prayed so many prayers—to ensure a solid relationship with Christ—that I lost count.

But one day I realized that my eternal destiny didn't depend on me. It depended on God's promises. I'm a visual person, so this truth didn't sink in until someone passed along a concrete illustration of ultimate security.

I knew the Bible said I was a sinner, and sin separated me from God (Romans 3:23). But that's why Jesus died on the cross—to pay for my sins—and if I accepted His gift of salvation, I could begin a Father-child relationship with Him (John 1:12). Then He came back to life, conquering death, to give *me* a new life, eternal life with Him (Romans 6:23).

Here's where the visual comes in: Jesus said,

> *I give them eternal life, and they will never perish.*
> *No one can snatch them away from me,*
> *for my Father has given them to me,*
> *and he is more powerful than anyone else.*
> *No one can snatch them from the Father's hand.*
> *The Father and I are one.*
> —John 10:28–30 (poetic arrangement mine)

From these three verses, I can now visualize Jesus holding me tightly in His hand so I can't fall out, and no one—and nothing—can wrench me out of His loving hand. Then God the Father is wrapping *His* all-powerful hand around the spike-scarred hand of Jesus in an unbreakable super-bond. This is the foundation of our intimacy with God.

On top of that I have my Father's promise: *He Himself has said, I will never leave you or forsake you* (Hebrews 13:5 HCSB).

So, yes, if we have accepted God's gift of salvation, the Lord is our rock-solid base, especially when we feel insecure. He is our strength when we feel weak. He is our hope when everything seems hopeless. And we can say (or write) with King David, *I cling to you; your strong right hand holds me securely* (Psalm 63:8). And we can pray,

> Oh, Lord, our Rock,
> You know our insecurities and shortcomings
> better than we know them ourselves.
> So please help us find our sure footing
> and our confidence in You.
> Even eternity holds no fears
> if we're trusting in You alone.

Journal Prompts

1. When have you felt insecure in the past? What kinds of things make you feel insecure? Jot a few notes on the next page.
2. If you have not yet found security in an intimately personal relationship with Christ, why not turn over the controls of your life to Him

right now? Give Him all your fears, anxieties, shortcomings, insecurities, doubts, pain—everything. You can pray—maybe even write out your prayer as a combination confession-and-confidence psalm—something like this:

Oh, God of heaven,
thank You for sacrificing Your perfect Son
to pay the penalty for my sin
and to rise again to give me new life in You.
I choose to trust Jesus alone
to wash me clean,
to be my Security,
and to welcome me Home someday
to be with You forever.
Thank You, Lord!
Amen.

3. If you already know Christ as Your Savior, visualize yourself in that double grip of Jesus and the Father. Make note of any insecurities you need to release. Then, when you're ready, write a confidence psalm, expressing your commitment to standing firm in your security in Christ.

_____
_____
_____
_____

JOYCE K. ELLIS

My sin—oh, the bliss of this glorious thought!—
My sin, not in part but the whole,
Is nailed to the cross, and I bear it no more,
Praise the Lord, praise the Lord, O my soul![20]
—Horatio G. Spafford (1828–1888)

Just as [people] spontaneously praise whatever they value, so they spontaneously urge us to join them in praising it: "Isn't she lovely? Wasn't that glorious?" ... I think we delight to praise what we enjoy because the praise not merely expresses but completes the enjoyment ... The delight is incomplete till it is expressed.[21]

—C. S. Lewis

11

FEELING JOYFUL

*I will praise you, Lord, with all my heart;
I will tell of all the marvelous things
you have done.
I will be filled with joy because of you.
I will sing praises to your name,
O Most High.*
—Psalm 9:1–2

Many years ago, the movie *Chariots of Fire* touched my heart. It's the true story of Eric Liddell, an Olympic runner known as the Flying Scotsman, who also happened to be on his way to becoming a missionary to China. In the 1924 Paris Olympics, he gold-medaled for Great Britain, but he disappointed his countrymen because his best event was scheduled for a Sunday. And Liddell remained steadfast to his personal convictions that he shouldn't run on a God-appointed day of rest.

His sister, also a missionary, questioned his participation in the Olympics at all because of his calling.

But Eric replied, "I believe God made me for a purpose—for China. But He also made me fast. And when I run, I feel His pleasure."

Eric Liddell found joy in being and doing what God created Him to be and do—and in *not* giving in to peer pressure. His example inspires me. I've discovered that "feeling His pleasure" is the best kind of joy there is.

Joy! (It's hard for me to write the word without an exclamation point after it.) Joy burrows deeper than happiness and bubbles up from within (see the next devotion). Jesus promises a special kind of joy in following Him and seeing Him again someday—and *no one can rob [us] of that joy* (John 16:22).

Joy is for sharing. We celebrate our joy about promotions on Linked In, wedding anniversaries on Facebook, new babies on Instagram. "Shared joy is a double joy"—says a Swedish proverb—"shared sorrow is half a sorrow."[22]

While sightseeing in other parts of the country or world, I often wish I could share the moment with family members and friends not present. That's why I take a lot of photos and videos. And I'm so grateful for phone cameras so I can share the experience on social media or later in person.

Similarly, if you're a sports fan and you see a great play on TV, you'll likely call a spouse or friend into the room to watch the instant replay with you. Shared enthusiasm exhilarates—whether it's for our home team, the beauty of God's creation, or answered prayer.

Not only does expressing praise with others complete our delight, as Lewis suggests (see beginning of this devotion), but it also becomes even richer when someone else joins us in the praise. And that's what writing psalms of praise and thanksgiving can do when we share them with others.

One time, King David's desperation grew so intense that, in order to escape the clutches of an enemy, King Abimelech, David pretended to be insane.[23]

Afterward, he wrote, *Come, let us tell of the Lord's greatness; let us exalt his name together* (Psalm 34:3).

In the first half of the verse, several other versions of Scripture use the word *magnify*. So we might paraphrase the verse this way: "Put God under a magnifying glass with me. Show Him off, bigger and greater than ever." When our vision of the great God of the universe dims, clouded by personal pain or global calamities, we often need other people who will hold out a magnifying glass and let us see His great character and love. So we can pray,

> Oh, Lord of All,
> I confess my overwhelming "me focus."
> And I confess my tendency
> to remember my disappointment
> more than Your care and grace.
> So, when I forget, please keep reminding me
> to "put You under a magnifying glass"
> so all can see what an awesome God You are!

Journal Prompts

How would you define *joy*? What is your greatest joy? Where do you feel God's pleasure? With whom do you share your joy? What joy in your life would you like to thank God for? You may want to start writing a thanksgiving psalm right now.

A thanksgiving psalm can be a praise psalm, thanking God for what He has done. See the example below:

> Lord, I can't remember the last time
> I thanked You for simple things:
> Thank You for a warm house
> on a scary-cold day.
> Thank You for the sun that peeked out today
> after an insufferable gray spell.
> Thank You for clothes to wear
> and shoes to protect my feet.
> Thank You for eyes to read Your Word,
>   ears to hear my family say, "I love you,"

a nose to smell gardenias and lilacs and honeysuckle,
   a mouth to sing Your praises,
   and the sense of touch to feel textures
   like sand and oceans and snow and spring grass.
 There's so much to thank You for. Why do I forget?
 Thank You, Lord, for all Your gifts—simple and grand!
 —Joyce K. Ellis

Or you might want to write a praise psalm that begins, "Father, I feel Your pleasure when …" Then praise Him for the joy you find in that.

_____
_____
_____
_____
_____
_____
_____
_____
_____
_____
_____
_____
_____
_____
_____
_____
_____
_____

Fun Frameworks

As we learn about our Lord from His Word, we can write psalms from our own experience and feelings. Our psalms can be quite simple—something like this praise psalm of mine:

> All my praise forever goes to my three-in-one God!
> I love You, Father, for adopting me as Your child.
> I love You, Jesus, for paying the awful price
> to cleanse me from my sin.
> I love you, Holy Spirit, for living within me,
>   comforting me,
>   and reshaping my confused prayers
>   before the Father.

We can write acrostic psalms, as some biblical psalm writers did. In Psalm 119, each stanza or line begins with a different letter of the Hebrew alphabet. Here's an example in English:

God's Word

Whispers of Your Wisdom join me
as I walk along Your pathway.
Options of Peace are the flowers
that bloom along the path's edges.
Restfulness comes while lingering long enough
to absorb the sights and sounds.
Distance between us diminishes
as I stop to ponder and wish only to stay.
—Kim Shackelford

Or we can write psalms that are lovely works of art, perhaps tying a contemporary theme to a biblical story. Here's an example from Luci Shaw, based on Luke 1:39–45:

Salutation

Framed in light,
Mary sings through the doorway.
Elizabeth's six-month joy
jumps, a palpable greeting,
a hidden first encounter
between son and Son.
And my heart turns over
when I meet Jesus
in you.[24]
—Luci Shaw

Enjoy all your options as you write your own psalms to God.

Joseph Bayly had to bury three sons during his lifetime—one an infant, one almost five years old, and one a teenager. Out of that life of pain and his intimate relationship with God, he wrote psalms of honesty that touch the soul. Psalms like the one on the next page.

A Psalm of Suffering

Lord you're the farmer
I'm your field
It is your right
to fence me in
to plow
my soul's hard ground
with furrows deep
to dig down far
for hidden rocks
to harrow hard
till soil is smooth
but only
if you plan
a harvest
of holiness.
—Joseph Bayly[25]

© 1987 Joseph Bayly. *Psalms of My Life* is published by David C. Cook. All rights reserved.

Pain insists on being attended to. God whispers to us in our pleasures, speaks in our conscience, but shouts in our pain: it is His megaphone to rouse a deaf world.[26]
—C. S. Lewis

12

FEELING PAIN

*I am worn out from sobbing.
All night I flood my bed with weeping,
drenching it with my tears.
My vision is blurred by grief...
The Lord has heard my plea;
the Lord will answer my prayer.*
—Psalm 6:6–7, 9

I am a pain wimp. There! I've admitted it in print. The timing of this chapter—and that hard-to-admit fact—couldn't be more apropos because I just came home from a dental appointment.

Pain—acute and chronic—seems to stalk me.

One night when our children were in the middle grades, we took them out for pizza. After a fun evening, we started driving home. I carried my usual to-go cup of Coke, which I quickly finished off.

Suddenly, one of the worst pains of my life punched me in the gut. I was grateful for that empty plastic cup. I lost everything I had just eaten. The horrific pain led to an ER visit and eventual diagnosis of pancreatitis (inflammation of the pancreas).

While in and out of the hospital for more than a month, dealing with the pain and inability to keep food down, the emotional pain of not being able to take care of my family also hit. Questions haunted me: What could I have done to cause this—or prevent it? How long will this agony last? Are the kids going to be okay?

No stranger to pain, I'm not sure which types are worse: physical or emotional, acute or chronic. But chronic physical pain literally wears me out and takes its toll emotionally and spiritually. So I have to be honest with God, the Great Physician, about my pain. He's the One who can heal heart and body—or help me endure, however long the pain will last.

Various hurts and sufferings fill the lament psalms Scripture has recorded for us. And we, too, can cry out to God in intimate honesty. We don't have to pretend in front of Him. He knows our pain. He feels it along with us. And He has plans for it. Otherwise, it wouldn't be happening.

We see the ultimate in heartrending communication on the cross. I imagine that during the anguish of spikes, thorns, and torn flesh, Jesus screamed at the top of His lungs, *"My God, My God, why have You forsaken me?"* (Mark 15:34 HCSB). Perhaps His final words sounded a different tone at a different volume. In ultimate acceptance and trust, He managed to say, *"Father, into Your hands I entrust my spirit"* (Luke 23:46 HCSB).

Then, after what seemed an interminable waiting period, came the *ultimate* answer: the angel at the empty tomb cried out, *"He isn't here! He is risen from the dead"* (Matthew 28:6).

But first came, "My God! Why?"

First, we spill out our weakness, our struggle, our wiped-out emotions. Then God has room to pour into us His strength. And eventually, we can cry, "I don't understand it, but I trust You anyway." And when we can see the transformation beginning, it might lead to incredible bursts of praise.

When we're in crisis mode, we can seldom see yesterday or tomorrow—only this moment. Our view of God is like looking through the wrong end of binoculars. What we'd hoped would magnify His presence, instead projects Him farther away.

We need a spiritual View-Master, of sorts. As we hold the viewer up to the Light, our minds click through the photo disc, slide after slide—vibrant, full-color, 3-D images—of His grace in past crises.

Often we can clarify our thoughts, writing a lament psalm in a format like this: Help! Enough! I trust You. I choose to praise You.

But it may take a while to get from the Help and Enough stages to the ones of trust and praise. Complaints spill out easier than words of confidence.

Although God graciously lets us start where we are, He longs for us to move forward, closer to Him. Eventually we can, through His supernatural enabling, come to a place of hope—a place of acceptance, trust, and, yes, even praise.

"David didn't deny the reality of his pain," write Randy Newman and Lin Johnson. "But he affirmed there is more to reality than complaining. We need to remember who God is. We need to recall His character.[27]

Our minds often block out past pain. But sometimes we also rub out the memory of who God is. We forget His comfort. We forget how often He has overcome the impossible. So our best prayer may be, "Lord, please help me remember."

Then we can come to that all-important turning point David captured this way: *Weeping may last through the night, but joy comes with the morning* (Psalm 30:5). So we can pray,

> Oh, God of all Comfort and Strength,
> We know that You are here with us—always present.
> But when we've been waiting so long for relief,
> we feel like we can't take any more pain.
> So please hold us tightly in Your loving embrace—
> and, in our pain, keep whispering, "I love You"
> until we can quit trying to wiggle free
> and trust You completely—even in this.

Journal Prompts

List one or more of the painful times, the hurtful times, the frustrating times, the impossible times of your past. Ask God to remind You how He brought you through it. Writing psalms about those experiences can help turn the binoculars around the *right* way.

_____
_____
_____
_____
_____
_____

OUR HEART PSALMS

What colorful contrasts David experienced: from wailing to dancing ... sounds of silence to songs of joy ... cynicism to caring, and from needing no one to trusting God. He exchanged a growing insecurity for unshakeable confidence. No wonder he vowed to praise the Lord and to give thanks to him forever![28]
—Don Wyrtzen

Don't Rush It!

As you begin writing a lament psalm to work through a current difficult situation or to find healing for a wound, don't rush to reach the praise segment. I doubt that any of the laments of Scripture were written in one sitting. I suspect that the psalmists often lived in the land of "Help!" for some time before they crossed over the bridge of "I trust You" in their relationship with God.

On the other hand, it's hard to see the Light when we choose to wallow face down in a mud puddle of self-pity. Invite God into whatever you're going through. And eagerly anticipate what He wants to do.

A Lament
(excerpts)

Lord, You appointed
> that I should cry, so that You might comfort;
> that I should fall, so that You might pick me up;
> that I should come to the brink of death, so that You might deliver me.

My God, You ordained
> that I be humbled by many blows,
> in order that You might protect me;
> that I be disciplined under Your heavy hand,
> in order that I might know Your love;
> that I be pounded by waves of grief,
> in order that I might trust in You.
> Almighty One, you established
> shadows to be my friends, that I might look for You;
> darkness to pursue me, that I might run after You;
> heaviness to close in on me, that I might flee to You.

God, my God, you decreed
pain for me,
that I should find that You alone bring comfort;
weariness,
that I might discover rest only in You;
> innumerable rejections, even from my friends,
>> that I might know that You alone ...
>> do not abandon,
>> and that only You are truly faithful
>> to those whom You love.

—Dr. Ardel B. Caneday

They want quick answers to the deepest questions of life and miss the value of those times of anxious waiting, seeking with patient uncertainties until the answers come. They lose the moment when the answers are revealed in dazzling clarity.[29]
—Dietrich Bonhoeffer

13

FEELING IMPATIENT

I am worn out, O Lord; have pity on me!
Give me strength; I am completely exhausted
and my whole being is deeply troubled.
How long, O Lord, will you wait to help me?
—Psalm 6:2–3 (GNT)

Sitting in the doctor's waiting room (an all-too-frequent occurrence), I noticed a familiar sign on the opposite wall: If you have been waiting more than 15 minutes beyond your appointment time, please talk to the receptionist.

I marvel at this new time-sensitivity phenomenon. Unlike years past, I seldom have to wait past my appointment time, and I appreciate the after-visit surveys' obsession with timeliness.

Waiting drives people crazy: checkout lanes, car repairs, amazon.com deliveries—especially at Christmastime.

Of course, rush-hour traffic is grossly misnamed because no one can rush anywhere in freeway gridlock. And often, when my husband sees a car weaving in and out of heavy traffic, he says, "That guy must think he's very important."

Impatience saturates our culture. Big things: we're impatient to receive a college scholarship notification or job offer, to find a good spouse, to get pregnant, to give birth, to see our children become less dependent on us, to receive medical test results. Small things: we're impatient to go home after a long workday, to get an elevator, to find a parking space.

Our impatience can span everything from waiting for the microwave to finish cooking our instant lunch to waiting for relief from a chronic malady or pain we've been dealing with for years.

In our impatience, we may shoot a quick prayer to heaven: "How long, Lord?" That's biblical. It's a question asked more than twenty times in the Psalms. Sometimes it seems like the Lord doesn't hear us, doesn't care, or isn't doing anything. But we're simply in God's waiting room—another familiar place to me regarding work, health, relationships, and more.

Impatience may stem from fear, pain, or insecurity. We're impatient in traffic because we fear being late for an important business appointment. We're impatient for our daughter to come home because we fear her car broke down in the snowstorm. We're impatient for a new medical treatment because we desperately need relief from our pain. We're impatient to find a mate because we may feel vulnerable or incomplete alone.

Chris Tiegreen offers this perspective: "In the moment, [God] seems to take an excruciatingly long time to work out his plan or to fulfill a promise ... But looking back after the fact, his timing usually makes sense. He knows how to build up to a moment and deliver when conditions are ripe. He is a masterful orchestrator of the divine plan."[30]

Waiting is not optional. How we wait makes the difference. And it starts with turning to the Lord. Scripture promises that our God hears us when we call out to Him. In the Psalms, His people often cry out for Him to hear them. David wrote, *Bend down, O Lord, and hear my prayer; answer me, for I need your help* (Psalm 86:1).

The writer of Psalm 116 expresses his confidence in this prayer-hearing, prayer-answering God: *I love the Lord because he hears my voice and my prayer for mercy.*

Remembering this, he says, *Because he bends down to listen, I will pray as long as I have breath!* (vv. 1–2).

When I'm in a doctor's waiting room, one thing that eases the waiting time is the plethora of paperwork I have to fill out. Never mind that the office already called me and asked me the same questions during preregistration, I have to rehash the information with pen and paper on a clipboard or with my index finger on an electronic tablet. But ultimately, *my* waiting time often depends on how much time the patient ahead of me needs with the doctor.

When we're in God's Waiting Room, we might consider what kinds of things God has to work out in other people's lives that will affect our waiting time and our answer.

But even more importantly, what might He want to accomplish in me through the waiting process? What self-assessment "paperwork," so to speak?

Psalm 46 encourages us to remember God's presence with us in the Waiting Room, to remember that He's in control. He says to us, *"Be still, and know that I am God!"* Then He puts everything in perspective with this ultimate promise: *"I* will *be honored"* (emphasis mine)—and who knows how far throughout the world He will receive honor in other patients' lives, so to speak, because of the waiting He is calling *us* to do?

David wrote, *Wait patiently for the Lord. Be brave and courageous. Yes, wait patiently for the Lord* (Psalm 27:14). So we can pray,

> Oh, God of Patience,
> sometimes it takes a lot of courage to wait,
> a lot of faith stretching,
> a lot of quieting our hearts before You,
> a lot of reminders of Your love.
> So please keep reminding us
> that You are here
> and You hear.
> You answer in Your time
> and in Your time You will be honored.

Journal Prompts

1. What are you waiting for? That question can be taken two ways:
   - What are some things you're patiently or impatiently waiting for? (List a few.)
   - What on earth are you waiting for? (Implied: Get at it! What steps does God want you to take while waiting for His answer?)

   Make some notes here about your God-sent Waiting-Room experience(s). What are some things He might want to do *in* you or *through* you during this time? For instance, could His plan include acceptance of the situation rather than deliverance from it?

2. When you're ready, write a psalm about time you've spent in God's Waiting Room. You could write any category of psalm, such as confession, thanksgiving, praise, or confidence. (See possible patterns in the appendix.)

OUR HEART PSALMS

JOYCE K. ELLIS

In the Beloved

"In the Beloved"[32] accepted am I,
Risen, ascended, and seated on high:
Saved from all sin thro' His infinite grace,
With the redeemed ones accorded a place.

"In the Beloved" I went to the tree
There, in His person, by faith I may see
Infinite wrath rolling over His head,
Infinite grace, for He died in my stead.

"In the Beloved," God's marvelous grace
Calls me to dwell in this wonderful place,
God sees my Savior and then He sees me
"In the Beloved," accepted and free.
—Civilla D. Martin (1866–1948)

OUR HEART PSALMS

O God, sometimes You seem so far away.
I cannot in this moment sense Your presence
or feel Your power.

The darkness enveloping me is stifling.
This depression is suffocating.
How long, O God, do I have to live in this void?
O God, how long?

Break into this black night, O God;
    fill in this vast emptiness.
Enter into my conflict
    lest I fall, never to rise again.

I continue to trust in Your ever-present love.
I shall again discover true joy
    in my relationship with You.
I will proclaim Your praises, my Lord,
    for You will never let me go.[31]
—Leslie Brandt

Psalm 13 from *Psalms/Now*, 3rd edition by Leslie F. Brandt 1974, 1996 Concordia Publishing House. Used with permission. www.cph.org.

Gratitude gets us through the hard stuff. To reflect on your blessings is to rehearse God's accomplishments. To rehearse God's accomplishments is to discover his heart. To discover his heart is to discover not just good gifts but the Good Giver. Gratitude always leaves us looking at God and away from dread. It does to anxiety what the morning sun does to valley mist. It burns it up.[33]
—Max Lucado

14

FEELING GRATEFUL FOR WHAT GOD HAS DONE

*I will praise you forever, O God,
for what you have done.
I will trust in your good name.*
—Psalm 52:9

I lay at the bottom of the stairs, dazed. I didn't remember falling, but there I was, lying on my back, staring at the ceiling. The first thing that crossed my mind was my mother's fall down stairs years earlier—her broken back, her years in a wheelchair.

But here I was—staying in the home of a missionary friend, Martha, in Guatemala—on day two of a four-week mission trip. I had gone upstairs to take a shower, and when I returned, I must have tripped.

Lying there, I started checking arms and legs to make sure everything functioned properly. And I cried out to God with all that was in me, *What now, Lord? Why now?*

All I could think of was the busy schedule ahead. In a huge stretch of faith, I had accepted a four-week challenge: one week of speaking and teaching, then one week with each of three successive short-term teams from our church. Clinics. Children's ministries. Interpreting. Wherever else I was needed.

Gingerly, I grabbed a nearby post and stood. A headache grew, along with a softball-sized bump on the back of my head. I couldn't deal with some kind of injury.

When Martha returned from errands, she applied an ice pack and called a doctor friend. He said that if I wasn't having any vision problems or nausea, I should be okay.

The next day's schedule included speaking for two events—both women's prayer groups. I awoke that morning, dizzy and foggy-brained. Martha said I could cancel, but we prayed, and the Lord nudged me to trust Him and move forward with the schedule.

I poured out my heart honestly to God. I was scared. But I soon realized that these concussion symptoms were another Red Sea moment. And I had seen before what God could do when I gave an "impossible" situation to Him.

When we arrived at the first event, the sight of a long flight of stairs to the meeting room made me nervous. But when we told the women what had happened, they prayed with me too. I felt a little wonky during the first part of the meeting, but then something remarkable happened. When it was time for me to speak, I had no balance problems. No headache. No foggy brain.

The same phenomenon happened each time I had a ministry opportunity during those four weeks. I was fine whenever I had a responsibility, but in between, the concussion symptoms returned. It seemed God was saying, "See? You still need Me."

I tell that story often because I love to give God the praise for what He did in that situation in 2015. I have never been more dependent on Him, and I have never seen Him work more dramatically.

As of this writing, I still experience concussion-symptom leftovers from time to time. And adjusting to my new normal has challenged me. But seeing how far I've come from those early days after the concussion strengthens my faith.

The psalm writer Asaph wrote, *"I cry out to God without holding back"*[34] (Psalm 77:1, emphasis mine). As I mentioned early in this book, King David taught that principle as well, paraphrased by Eugene Peterson this way: *Never hide your feelings from him* (Psalm 34:5 MSG).

No matter what pain or joy we're traveling through, we can cry out to God, openly confessing our feelings, knowing how precious we are to Him. He sees. He delivers.

We may write a lament psalm about the crisis. Then later we can begin our thanksgiving psalm where our laments left off. The combination of these two psalm types must delight our God, who sees—and delivers. God says, *"Giving thanks is a sacrifice that truly honors me"* (Psalm 50:23). So we can pray,

> Oh, Always-in-Control Father,
> Your infinite love and care for us astounds us.
> No matter what we say to try to thank You,
> it all seems so inadequate.
> So please help us express what we can
> and trust Your loving heart to understand.

Journal Prompts

1. Think about a difficult situation the Lord has brought you through—one about which you can now praise Him. Make notes about it here or go ahead and start writing a lament psalm about it—however short or long you wish. Can you include a turning point, where you at least see a little hope or you choose to trust Him?
2. Make notes about the way you came through that situation, and/or write a thanksgiving psalm about it. Remember, thanksgiving psalms often have their roots in lament psalms. See how these ideas can mesh in the biblical patterns below.

Praise and Thanksgiving psalms (contrasted with laments)

Lament psalms say	Thanksgiving psalms say
	Praise the Lord
Help!	I cried out for help
Enough!	This is how bad it was
I trust You	I trusted You; You did it
I choose to praise You	I promised to praise You, so I praise You now

Tearful Heart

A lament psalm
written after a previous personal crisis

Oh, Lord, I can hardly breathe
from the steady torrent of tears I can't seem to shut off.
I'm so tired of crying,
but everything I try to do yields to weeping,
weeping, unending weeping.
My swollen eyes can't focus.
My heart weighs so heavy in my chest
for my pride, my fear,
my difficulty in trusting You for the outcome.
I can scarcely see this page through my tears.
But I know You're here,
and I pray that You'll give me what I need to function.
I can't sit around and cry all day,
no matter how much I'm hurting.
May Your Spirit make sense of my prayers.
You are my Rock, my peace.
I can't give in to this emotional upheaval.
Take over. Take care of me
because I certainly don't know how to take care of myself.
Help me to trust You one more time.
And my praises will be Yours forever.
—Joyce K. Ellis

JOYCE K. ELLIS

My Father of Grace
A thanksgiving psalm
written after the lament on the previous page

Oh, Lord, my Rock, my peace—
when emotions choked me,
tears persisted,
and neither mind nor eyes could focus,
I cried out to You in my stress
in my distress
I begged You to help me trust You
one more time.
And You did.
You rescued me from paralyzing fears,
and now You're redecorating life
with the tranquility of Your own heart.
How can I ever stop praising You
for Your grace that heals, mends, restores,
gives me hope, gives me joy?
How can I ever stop praising You
for Your unfailing love,
for Your overflowing mercy?
Let everyone who has ever seen Your loving, mighty hand
rejoice and praise Your name!
—Joyce K. Ellis

Ultimately, the goal in writing our heart psalms is honesty. The psalmists of Scripture exulted in victories, thrilled at new understandings of God's creation and character, confessed rage over injustices (especially those affecting them personally), and even told God what they thought He should do in no uncertain terms. But this honesty nestles within an intimate personal relationship with our Creator God and our Loving Savior, the Lord Jesus Christ.

We may be compelled to conclude that our fear, anxiety, dread, apprehension, worry is a simple lack of confidence in God's power to strengthen us to do what he has asked us, humanly challenging though it may be. Can we doubt that God will allow whatever is best for us to come into our life?[35]
—Luci Shaw

15

FEELING WORRIED

I believed in you, so I said,
"I am deeply troubled, Lord."
In my anxiety [worry] I cried out to you.
—Psalm 116:10–11 (brackets mine)

Worry doesn't own me, but I confess I dabble in it from time to time.

I held it together the day we drove our oldest offspring to his first year of college—three hours away. I held it together as we settled him into the dorm and met his roommates. I even held it together fairly well as we drove home.

But the next day, as I sat in church with the rest of our family, singing songs of worship, I lost it. Loneliness hit. Tears flowed. What-ifs crowded out peace. Worries assaulted my thoughts.

Why is it most of the things we worry about never happen? Our son did fine. So much needless worry.

So much unnecessary wear and tear on the emotions.

I don't consider myself a chronic worrier. But when trials seem overwhelming, when a much-needed check doesn't arrive, when bad circumstances keep worsening, when I find myself in a jam I don't know how to get out of, when I face "the impossible," I worry. Once in a while. Maybe. At times. Okay, more often than I like to admit. I suspect many people do. That makes me feel better, but worry isn't good for us.

Sometimes I don't recognize worry in myself. It takes a diagnosis from my husband, a friend, or Scripture itself.

Perhaps David had a blind spot about worry as well. To a certain extent, in Psalm 139, he may be asking God to help him identify worry in his life: *"Search me, O God, and know my heart; test me and know my anxious thoughts"* (v. 23). Perhaps that verse is a good prayer for identifying worry we may not recognize.

Other times, we feel our worries deeply. We can't seem to turn them off during the day, and they keep us awake at night.

From the time I read Corrie ten Boom's book, *The Hiding Place,* and later saw the movie, her life story has captivated me. This Dutch woman ended up in a Nazi concentration camp because her family hid Jews in their home. In one of her books, Corrie discusses the topic of worry and relates this story: "Bishop Quayle ... who must have had a keen sense of humor ... told of a time when he sat up late in his study, worrying over many things. Finally the Lord came to him and said, 'Quayle, you go to bed. I'll sit up the rest of the night.'" [36]

Ultimately, Corrie learned these important truths about worry: (1) "Worry is a cycle of inefficient thoughts whirling around a center of fear"[37]; (2) "Worry does not empty tomorrow of its sorrow, it empties today of its strength."[38]

Jesus taught that worrying doesn't help anything. We may have read or heard this passage so often that it doesn't sink in anymore, but read these excerpts again, thoughtfully, and let Jesus' words sink in: "*'I tell you not to worry ... Can all your worries add a single moment to your life? ... Don't worry about these things ... Seek the Kingdom of God above all else ... and he will give you everything you need ... Don't worry about tomorrow, for tomorrow will bring its own worries. Today's trouble is enough for today'*" (Matthew 6:25–34).

My friend Jane Rubietta calls worry the "wrinkled brow disease." And I love her visual image of the antidote for worry—Jesus Himself, "who pats his lap, holds out beckoning hands, and says, 'Shhh. Shhh. Come. Sit. Look at me, looking at you, loving you.'"[39]

If your mind is stuck in a worry-thoughts playlist, replace those faith-debilitating song titles with new ones:

1. Our God Is the God of the Impossible
2. Nothing Is Too Hard for the God of the Impossible
3. God Is with Me (as a believer in Jesus Christ), Even If I Can't Feel His Presence
4. God Is Working Even When I Can't See What He's Doing
5. I Can Trust the God of the Impossible
6. Waiting for His Perfect Timing Will Be Worth It

Hit the Shuffle button, then Repeat All.

Let's shape our worries into heart psalms: *Instead of worrying, pray. Let petitions and praises shape your worries into prayers, letting God know your concerns ... It's wonderful what happens when Christ displaces worry at the center of your life* (Philippians 4:6–7 MSG).

When can we say, "This is too hard for God"? Never! So we can pray,

> Oh, God of the Impossible,
> sometimes it's hard to let go of our worries.
> They've been familiar friends too long.
> So please keep reminding us
> that the burden only increases
> when we try to carry tomorrow's troubles
> along with today's.

Journal Prompts

1. For novelists, the words *what if* are golden. They open numerous plot possibilities—the worse, the better. But for the Christian, what-ifs assault our faith. And faith and worry are mutually exclusive. Are there particular worries that dominate your thoughts in the daytime and then prevent sleep at night? Make notes about them below. Where are you in the course of processing them?
2. If you haven't admitted to God your lack of faith in His power, you might want to begin a confession psalm. If you're ready to create a new playlist for your mind and affirm your trust that God is in control, perhaps you can start working through your thoughts to create a confidence psalm.

A possible pattern for confession psalms (patterned after Psalm 51)

cry for mercy
call sin sin (specificity)
admit our sin nature
acknowledge God's holiness
repent, seek cleansing and a restored relationship
profess confidence in God
promise God your praise

A possible pattern for confidence psalms (variable, often include these elements)

affirmation of the trustworthiness of God
reasons for confidence
reality of crisis or things that cause you to be fearful
assurance of God's presence
promise of future help or eternal hope

OUR HEART PSALMS

Sovereign

When I reflect on Your awesome sovereignty,
> in my frailty I ask—
>> Who is like You, O God?
>> Who can grasp the hurricane in one's hand,
>>> or harness the turbulent winds of a tornado?
>> Who can stop the surging sea,
>>> or reverse the river's current?
>> Who is able to straighten what You, O God, have made twisted,
>>> or who can account for the things You have left lacking?
>> Who has power over the day of one's death,
>>> or who is able to add an hour to one's life?

As I meditate upon Your word, O Lord,
> You instruct me …
>> No one can fathom Your sovereign plan
>>> from beginning to end.
>> Whatever Your mighty hand moves to accomplish
>>> is done without being thwarted.
>> Whatever You purpose to fulfill
>>> is realized without resistance from anyone.
>> For You, O Lord, are the almighty God,
>>> the God Who shall judge all things.

Therefore I bow in humble worship,
> I acknowledge You as my God.

—Dr. Ardel B. Caneday

Praise is the ... radiant splendor of the believer in the God of reality. One who is rightly related to the Lord of glory, and who thinks rightly of that relationship, cannot but adore Him with all that is within ... We ... must respond to Him in great praise.[40]
—Ronald B. Allen

16

FEELING WORSHIPFUL

*Worship the Lord in all his holy splendor.
Let all the earth tremble before him.*
—Psalm 96:9

I'll never forget the day I saw one of our grandchildren being born. It had been more than two decades since I gave birth to our own three offspring. Of course, I was a little preoccupied on those occasions.

But knowing all that has transpired for the previous nine months under the mother's protective care, how can anyone watch the miraculous birth of a baby—and not spontaneously praise God?

What a privilege to serve on the welcoming committee for a newborn! That tiny, vulnerable body emerged from a cocoon of warmth into a room 20 degrees colder. Squalling. Screaming, "Noooooooo!"

Long ago, David the psalm writer surely had seen the birthing of lambs in his care when he served as a shepherd. At some point, pondering the miracle of new life, a sense of wonder welled up within him, which led to a praise psalm, worshiping our Creator. David writes these words of adoration to God:

> *You made all the delicate, inner*
> *parts of my body*
> *and knit me together in my mother's womb.*
> *Thank you for making me so*
> *wonderfully complex!*
> —Psalm 139:13–14

What else fills our hearts with wonder and worship?

For me: amazing, timely answered prayers. Viewing the Grand Canyon in person. Hearing a beautiful cello concerto. And most importantly, understanding that God's fantastic plan of salvation included me. Those are a few from my list. What about yours?

God longs for us to worship Him everywhere and often. He deserves our constant praise. Admittedly, that comes more naturally on some days than on others. As I've said before, I can't always start my prayers with praise or worship, but I try to get to that point of praise before I leave my quiet place—at least with a brief note of gratitude that He is in control.

Some praise psalms—hymn psalms—focus exclusively on God and His character traits or attributes. We can praise God that He is holy, eternal, all-knowing, all-wise, all-powerful, ever-faithful, merciful, and sovereign (in control) over everything. He is a God of unfailing love, unfathomable grace, infinite wisdom—and so much more. In fact, because He is infinite, each of His characteristics is infinite.

But how can we mere mortals express praise to such an awesome God? (I confess my annoyance at the persistent overuse of *awesome* these days. If a piece of pie or a movie or a particular flavor of potato chip is awesome, what superlative do we have for our Creator and Savior, who truly inspires awe?)

A little-known psalm writer in Scripture, Ethan, wrote this: *The highest angelic powers stand in awe of God. He is far more awesome than all who surround his throne* (Psalm 89:7).

Listing God's attributes can be impressive. And the Psalms do that sometimes. But fleshing out that laundry list with experiences, specificity, and stories creates a warmer, personal, more intimate portrait of praise.

Psalms of worship grow out of our intimacy with God—a close encounter of the most personal kind. And our journey with the Father and with our Lord Jesus Christ gives us so much to write about. As the apostle John put it, *If they were all written down, I suppose the whole world could not contain the books that would be written* (John 21:25). A hymn psalm finds its roots in that deepening intimacy. So we can pray,

> Oh, Awesome Creator and Savior,
> You're in a class by Yourself.
> How could our puny praise ever describe
> Your indescribable worth?
> Yet You long to hear us try—
> to remember Who You are and to adore You for it.
> So please help us shift our focus from earthly concerns
> to Your infinite greatness
> and to draw closer to You.

Journal Prompts

What fills your heart with wonder and worship? While some hymn psalms in Scripture celebrate several of God's attributes, others focus on one. Most fall under the headings of God's goodness, majesty, or greatness.

Each of God's attributes means something different to you than it would to anyone else because of the way *you* personally have experienced it in your interaction with God. Now is your opportunity to praise Him from your exploration and discovery of His character. Make some notes here about your amazing God. If you're ready to write your own psalm, you might want to use this common pattern for praise or hymn psalms:

Introduction or call to praise:
> Examples:
>> Great is the Lord, and most worthy of praise
>> Come praise the Lord with me
>> Hallelujah
>> Praise the Lord

Body: Here's why—reasons to praise, usually beginning with the words *for* or *because*

Restatement of call to praise or further words of praise (optional)

_____

_____

_____

_____

_____

_____

*Jesus! I am resting, resting
In the joy of what Thou art;
I am finding out the greatness
Of Thy loving heart.*[41]
—Jean Sophia Pigott

Suffering

A wisdom psalm (excerpts)

Suffering is inevitable ...
> Bury yourself in the Word so you'll be strengthened and ready for suffering when it comes.

God has a purpose for our suffering, and it is for our good.
> Look for what He wants to teach you or reveal about Himself.

God ... can choose to end our trial at any time or choose to let it continue and walk with us through it ...
> Respect His right to do whatever He pleases in your life. He knows the big picture. We don't ...

We learn and grow more in times of suffering than in times of ease.
> Spend time reflecting on God's character, on how the Lord is changing you, and on what you are learning about Him ...

Suffering's goal is to make us more like Jesus ...
> It can smooth away some of our rough edges. This is desirable ...

Jesus completely understands our suffering and pain.
> He who suffered for us on the cross intercedes for us before God's throne. He helps us. He will never forsake us.

All suffering comes to an end.
> The Father promises that in a little while He Himself will restore you and make you strong, firm, and steadfast (1 Peter 5:10). Realistically, sometimes death brings the end to our suffering. In either case, we can look ahead in hope.

—Doreen Stewart

God must think it's okay to gripe [to Him] since He's given us so many examples of how to do it ... The authors of lament psalms were brutally honest with God. Yet somehow they reflected a healthy emotional and spiritual vigor ... These texts provide powerful lessons to aid us in spiritual and emotional maturity.[42]
—Randy Newman with Lin Johnson

17

FEELING ATTACKED

*Though a mighty army surrounds me,
my heart will not be afraid.
Even if I am attacked,
I will remain confident.*
—Psalm 27:3

A business deal gone bad: that's one way to describe it. The company run by people who claimed to be Christians had a good reputation when I entered into a contract with them. But little by little, I witnessed and heard about unsound business practices, unwise—if not illegal—actions, and more.

Although I had an open-ended contract, when I tried to pull out of the business deal, the company accused me of conspiring to sully their reputation. Employees became verbally abusive. They also spread lies about me, which could ruin *my* reputation, business, and ministry.

I attempted to *deflect anger* with *a gentle answer* (Proverbs 15:1) and not let them draw me into the fray. But their inexplicable, vitriolic attacks kept replaying in my mind, making it hard to concentrate during the day or rest at night. The Enemy's fingerprints were all over the situation. The battle exhausted me.

Although it took every ounce of strength I could draw from the Lord, I prayed for my attackers and others caught in this company's web. Each night my husband prayed for God's protection over my mind. I recited every Scripture I had memorized, it seemed, until I finally fell asleep. But sometimes that took several hours.

One day, during my time with the Lord, I read 2 Thessalonians 3:3: *The Lord is faithful, and he will strengthen you and keep you safe from the Evil One* (GNT). In those words, I heard God's personal, loving reassurance as clearly as if it were audible. I had known the truth of that verse, but here it was in black and white, just when I needed it.

As a memory aid, I visualized the two key phrases in that verse—*strengthen* (the image of my biceps on steroids to fight) and *keep you safe* or *protect you* (the image of God's all-powerful arms tented over my head to shelter me). I recited that verse over and over every night. Reminding myself of all the ways God had shown Himself *faithful* in my life over the years, I claimed His *strength* for the battle and *protection* over my mind—as well as my ministry and finances. Little by little, sleep came a bit more easily.

Several painful months passed before those haunting thoughts left me. As I tried to untangle myself from the company, its employees sabotaged my efforts to take my business elsewhere. But with the prayer support of a few carefully chosen confidants and with the absolute assurance that God is infinitely stronger than the Enemy, I finally broke free. That ordeal became yet another Red Sea experience. Once again, God showed His faithfulness and tutored me in trusting Him—in every situation.

Almost every lament psalm of Scripture depicts adversaries stalking the psalm writers to varying degrees. When I was younger, I couldn't relate to their predicament. But since then, I have cringed in the face of human conflict.

I have many nonhuman enemies too. Paul tells us that *our battle is not against flesh and blood, but against the rulers, against the authorities, against the world powers of this darkness, against the spiritual forces of evil in the heavens* (Ephesians 6:12 HCSB).

When I remembered that truth, I could better identify with the psalm writers' complaints about enemies. We can gripe to God about the Enemy with a capital *E*—and his army of evil underlings who delight in tripping us up spiritually. Our Creator is the only One who can do anything about it.

What about other enemies?

- time constraints and overscheduling
- circumstances I can't control (such as weather, accidents, interruptions, and other people's actions)
- my own weaknesses and limitations

Psalms in which the writers asked God to take vengeance on their enemies are called imprecatory psalms. *Imprecatory* means calling down curses or invoking evil. But Jesus introduced new principles for His kingdom—principles grounded in His love. The Sovereign God of the Universe tells us to give Him these enemy-attack situations and let Him take care of them. Enough said. So we can pray,

> Oh, our Protector God,
> we know how ugly human
> and nonhuman attacks can be.
> They can jar us into self-protect mode,
> devastate our faith,
> and inhibit our obedience to You.
> We feel so fragile and vulnerable.
> So please protect us with Your Spirit's armor.
> Help us stand up to the Enemy
> in Your strength
> and let You fight for us.

Journal Prompts

1. Make note here of any times when you have felt under attack from other people, daily pressures, or spiritual forces. Include any Scriptures that helped you through that time or anything the Lord taught you through it. When you're ready, write a psalm of your choosing—lament, thanksgiving, confidence, or praise—being honest with God about your before-and-after feelings. (See patterns and elements of each type in the appendix.)

A Mighty Fortress
A hymn psalm by Martin Luther
(translated from German by F. H. Hedge)

A mighty fortress is our God,
A bulwark never failing;
Our helper He, amid the flood
Of mortal ills prevailing,
For still our ancient foe
Doth seek to work us woe
His craft and pow'r are great,
And, armed with cruel hate,
On earth is not his equal.

Did we in our own strength confide,
Our striving would be losing;
Were not the right Man on our side,
The Man of God's own choosing.
Doth ask who that may be?
Christ Jesus, it is He;
Lord Sabaoth* His name,
From age to age the same,
And He must win the battle.

*Note: *Lord Sabaoth* refers to Almighty God, commander of the armies of heaven and earth, who went with Israel into battle and "led them to certain victory over the worshippers of ... false gods." [43]

The One Who's in Control
A confidence psalm

The whole world seems out of control sometimes.
The violence. The vitriol. The vindictiveness.
I dare not claim to know Your mind, Father,
but there are days when I think You, Lord of all,
are allowing us to go through difficult days
here on earth
so we'll be less enchanted with this life,
so we'll long more deeply for You
and for that day we get to live at Home with You.
Your Presence. Your perfection. Your peace.
Keep reminding me that You are in control.
Our hope is in You.
—Joyce K. Ellis

*Psalm 22 encourages us to take
our questions,
our complaints,
and our anger to God …
The starting point
is the desperate cry
of one who feels
abandoned by God,
betrayed by friends,
and battered by life.
Then the psalm suggests
that we remember what God has
done for us in the past.*[44]
—James Limburg

We can and usually do choose or will to be angry. Anger first arises spontaneously. But we can actively receive it and decide to indulge it, and we usually do.[45]
—Dallas Willard

18

FEELING ANGRY

Stop being angry!
Turn from your rage!
Do not lose your temper—
it only leads to harm.
—Psalm 37:8

When terrorists attacked the World Trade Center and the Pentagon on 9/11, I took it personally. I dare say most Americans did—even if they didn't know anyone wounded or killed in the calamity. When my husband and I learned an acquaintance we hadn't seen for years was among the victims, our grief and anger intensified. An attack on our country amounted to an attack on each of us. Yes, we felt anger.

Anger can pounce on us or creep into our hearts in many ways:

- anger at ourselves for mistakes or failures
- anger at others for hurting us or breaking a promise

- anger at God for not healing, not answering, or not intervening in a devastating situation.

Anger triggers can range from trivial everyday irritations to the inexcusable. But generally, it's motivated by *self*. Anger can be self-preservation boiling up in response to a threat against us or someone we love. Anger can stem from unmet expectations, unfair treatment, and unplanned-for dilemmas. It can result from someone's unconscious action that hurt us or from an intentional personal attack (though it may be unintentional far more often than we think).

Caution: anger can signal *danger* (*anger* with a *d* in front of it). Angry actions can escalate quickly, especially in personal conflicts. And each time angry words spill out, don't they become a little easier to say?

Anger can be like a magnet, picking up and hanging on to other harmful emotions, attitudes, and actions along the way. When our children were small and our house was burglarized, I felt violated, and my anger picked up fear, resentment, and doubt.

Sometimes anger accelerates, leading to bitterness, hatred, depression, and a desire (or even an attempt) to strike back.

Is anger sin? According to Scripture, no—not in itself. The Psalms include numerous verses about the anger of God, who is holy, sinless. And Jesus, Himself sinless, displayed anger on occasion.

In addition, David writes, *Don't sin by letting anger control you* (Psalm 4:4). But if we choose to let anger control us, rule over us, that constitutes sin.

So what do we do with the natural emotion of anger that attacks (and hounds) us in varying degrees of intensity? How do we keep anger from wandering across the boundary into sin?

I admit that sometimes I have stormed out of the house in anger—not a wise move, especially when Minnesota's winter has arrived. Sometimes I've harbored anger for a long time—not a wise move when anger can cause our minds and bodies to self-destruct. Sometimes I have allowed anger to harm relationships—also not a wise move when God calls us to love each other for our protection and joy. One of anger's worst consequences is that it robs us of His joy.

So how can we manage our anger in a way that pleases God?

He wants us to express our hearts honestly to Him. Wouldn't it be better to acknowledge how we feel about the situation and the people who have attacked our sense of well-being? Then if we turn all those feelings over to God, we give Him the opportunity to handle them as He sees fit.

After all, Paul instructs us, *Never take revenge. Leave that to the righteous anger of God. For the Scriptures say, "I will take revenge; I will pay them back," says the Lord* (Romans 12:19).

And how much better to acknowledge our feelings openly to the only One who can do anything about them. It's foolish to ignore them, cover them up, or take matters into our own hands and plunge ourselves into worse trouble.

Some hurts run deep and need significant time to heal. But one of the best healing treatments for the anger that exceeds normal emotion is forgiveness—forgiving ourselves when we've blown it, and forgiving others for intentional or unintentional hurts. Remember Jesus' words on the cross, *"Father, forgive them"*? Is the cause of my anger worse than the torture Jesus endured at that moment?

In another devotion, I quoted Luci Shaw's words: "Feel the fear and do it anyway." Perhaps we could adopt a similar mind-set regarding anger: Feel the anger and let it go anyway. In doing so, we'll find freedom. So we can pray,

> Oh, Forgiving Father,
> You have equipped us with emotions,
> which serve Your divine purpose.
> But when we allow them to overstep their boundaries,
> they're a danger to us and others.
> So please help us to be honest with You
> about our anger, humbly ask for forgiveness,
> and extend the same to those who anger us—
> all to deepen our loving relationship with You.

Journal Prompts

1. If the Lord has brought to mind a situation in which your anger has moved beyond simple emotion to sinful response, make notes about it here. Be cryptic if you're concerned about privacy. Begin writing a confession psalm to remove any barrier between you and a deep intimacy with your loving Savior.
2. If you harbor anger at yourself, someone else, or even the Lord for some deep hurt, let it go—through confession, forgiveness, and a wise response. In the second part of Psalm 4:4, David tells us, basically, to think through an anger-producing situation overnight and be quiet—presumably until we know how God wants us to respond. If you have gone through

this cycle, try writing a praise, thanksgiving, or confidence psalm about the process and note what He is teaching you.

OUR HEART PSALMS

In a modern-day lament psalm that Linnea Fellows wrote, she started where she was emotionally. She asked God questions of desperation. (Questions are often our first response.) Her honest pleadings expose raw, honest, even shocking emotions. Maybe you can identify with this excerpt:

> How could this happen? Don't You care about us at all?
> How dare You call Yourself "Love" and let this happen?
> How will we ever go on?

As she works through this faith crisis in the rest of her lengthy psalm, she acknowledges that God is her only help, and she reaches the point where she affirms her trust in Him:

> You are the God who knows …
> the best emotional place for me
> right now.
> I love You, Lord, and I trust You …
> —Linnea Fellows

A Psalm in Mojave Desert

I said
this desert land is barren
void of life and beauty.
I drive for miles
see nothing
only sand and sage
feel nothing
only wind and heat
taste nothing
but spit dried spit.
He said
have you ever driven
in spring
through this same desert
seen blossoms flower
gorgeous wild?
It's all a thing of timing.
Seeds of beauty
are there now hidden
waiting fall of rain
to bring them life.
Lord send rain
upon my world
my life
I'm tired of dried spit.[46]
—Joseph Bayly

© 1987 Joseph Bayly. *Psalms of My Life* is published by David C. Cook. All rights reserved.

*Those who honestly confront
their doubts often find themselves
growing into a faith
that transcends the doubts.*[47]
—Philip Yancey

19

FEELING DOUBTFUL

*When doubts filled my mind,
your comfort gave me renewed hope and cheer.*
—Psalm 94:19

A personal problem had been hanging over me for months—clouding my thoughts and provoking fears. I prayed and prayed. I believed I could trust God, but He didn't seem to be doing anything. The Lord answered other prayers but not this one. I didn't sense He had even heard me.

One night, as I prepared for bed, a thought flashed through my brain and lingered just long enough to disturb me: What if God isn't answering you because He isn't there—or doesn't care? What if everything you've always believed about Him is a lie?

Where did that come from?

Obviously, not from the Lord. As someone who began a faith relationship with God decades ago, I should be immune to thoughts like that, right? Yet there it was. And, with it, a load of guilt.

The faith-doubt tug of war isn't new. Doubt is one of the Enemy's favorite tools: *"Did God really sssssay?"* the Enemy hissed in the garden of Eden. (So am I handing the Enemy a victory when I *believe* him and *doubt* God?)

Many believers have been blindsided by doubt. Scripture examples abound. The disciples—moments from going down with their fishing boat in a fierce storm—heard their Master say, *"Don't be afraid ... Take courage. I am here!"* (Matthew 14:27). Then Peter literally tried to walk on water to reach Jesus, crying out to the Lord to save him. As Jesus pulled him into the boat, I imagine the Lord shaking His head. *"You have so little faith ... Why did you doubt me?"* (v. 31).

On another occasion, a dad who asked Christ to heal his son struggled between faith and doubt right in front of Jesus: *"I do believe! Help my unbelief"* (Mark 9:24 HCSB).

So what do we do when doubts sucker punch us?

My grandfather often said, "Never doubt in the shadows what the Lord has shown you in the light."[48]

In other words, "Remember the Red Sea!" (See chapter 2.)

Writing our heart psalms helps us record what the Lord has shown us in the light. We're back to recalling Red Sea moments—times when we've seen God answer us, show us His power, or comfort us during distress.

Doubts may come as fleeting questions or endurance-challenging plagues. They can crash down on us, resulting from fears or attacks, from feeling abandoned or unappreciated, and more. But Scripture's psalm writers have demonstrated God-sanctioned ways to cry out to Him—and keep crying out to Him—while we're in His Waiting Room.

In Psalm 27, David seems to whirl through a faith-doubt cycle. In my mind, the cycle might sound something like this: Oh, Lord, You're so wonderful. Why would I ever be afraid? Even if someone should attack me, I'll keep trusting You ... Oh, no! Help! Don't leave me when I'm under attack! ... Wait, are you still listening, Lord? ... I'm afraid. The battle's getting violent! ... Okay, settle down, self. Be brave while you wait for the Lord's answer.

But cycles of faith and doubt can be part of the *all things work together* promise of Romans 8:28. Max Lucado puts it this way: "God [is] the Master Weaver. He stretches the yarn and intertwines the colors, the ragged twine with the velvet strings, the pains with the pleasures. Nothing escapes his reach. Every king, despot, weather pattern, and molecule are at his command. He passes the shuttle back and forth across the generations, and as he does, a design emerges. Satan weaves; God reweaves."[49]

What a vivid visual!

I still haven't seen God's resolution to the problem that induced the guilt-producing doubt attack. And I've felt other sucker punches of doubt before and since. But remembering Red Sea moments strengthens my confidence that no matter what happens, we, as believers in Christ, can always trust our loving, all-wise, all-powerful God to do what's best.

Our faith doesn't rest on our lack of doubt but on the character of the God we have come to know. He is our comfort and cheer. So we can pray,

> Oh, God of Infinite Love and Patience,
> You welcome us to express our doubts
> but You also gently ask us to examine
> why we're doubting.
> So please remind us of all You've done for us
> and infuse us with the strength we need
> to shatter Enemy-sent doubts and lies.

Journal Prompts

1. Make note below of truths the Lord has shown you in the light that you can draw upon in the shadows or darkness. Do a search in a Bible app for appropriate Scripture verses, write them out, and memorize them so you can recall them during times of doubt.
2. If you're going through a faith-doubt cycle right now, start writing a lament psalm (that could eventually turn into a confidence psalm). Ask God for clarity in assessing the situation. Honestly express the doubts you feel and why. In His Waiting Room, continue to cry out to Him—in faith.

_____
_____
_____
_____
_____
_____
_____
_____
_____
_____
_____
_____

From Doubt to Praise

How long will my daughter fear?
I try to point her to You, but her fears loom ever larger.
Sometimes it seems easier to try to handle things myself
than to risk trusting You
and hear only silence.
But I can't do it alone.
I am not enough for her.
So I give my daughter to You with all her fears.
And I give You all my questions and doubts.
I trust that You have a good purpose in this for her and for us,
even though I don't see it now.
I have known Your faithfulness
and been comforted by Your Word.
Accomplish Your work in us, Lord.
I praise You for Your sovereign hand in our lives.
You are loving in all You do or bring to us.
You are right and good to do so.
I praise You.
—Doreen Stewart

Gratitude is a spiritual virtue that opens the door of the soul to the world around us. It creates a centrifugal force that causes the individual to look away from the self to God and to fellow human beings.[50]
—C. Hassell Bullock

20

FEELING GRATEFUL FOR WHAT WE HAVE

I said to the Lord, "You are my Master!
Every good thing I have comes from you."
—Psalm 16:2

As my husband pulled our car into a downtown parking garage space on a freezing winter day, a man in the next space exited his vehicle. On his feet he wore only flip-flops, so I assumed he was another of those audacious Minnesotans (I'm not a native—I just live here), trying to prove how hardy they are in subzero temps.

Then I noticed his beat-up car, stuffed with probably every possession he owned. He left before we got out of our car. But my judgmental attitude stabbed me deeply. How easily I judge people when I know nothing of their circumstances. How familiar I become with what I have and forget what others don't have.

I can't explain why our heavenly Father, in His sovereignty, allows vast inequities. What I do know is that He would like to hear me thank Him more often for His gifts—however great or small. Not only the material but also the spiritual.

Scripture reminds us of our spiritual inheritance—if we have given our lives to the Lord Jesus Christ. He has made us His children, His heirs along with Jesus, members of His family. He has given us His forgiveness, His Holy Spirit, His grace, His unfailing love, the precious assurance that He will never leave us.

He has given us His inexplicable peace and His all-sufficient strength to get us through anything. He has given us His promise that we'll be with our Savior the moment we say goodbye to this world. And so much more.

How can we forget to thank Him for all this? Yet we do.

Journaling my private times with the Lord has helped me slow down long enough to think about God's gracious gifts. He has given me so much.

God owes me nothing. I owe Him everything.

While journaling, no matter how hurt or frustrated I feel, I try to remember to thank Him for something. Even during difficult challenges, I can acknowledge everyday gifts:

- to be able to talk with Him
- to hold a pen and write out my thoughts
- to know—on the authority of His Word—that He never leaves me.

My list could go on forever.

I've come to love the reminders and repetition of Psalm 136. It's a psalm of thanks in an interesting format. The anonymous psalmist begins each section with *Give thanks to* _____. He fills in the blank with a different name or attribute of God, often elaborating on it. Then he recounts numerous reasons to thank Him. After each, he repeats the refrain: *[God's] faithful love endures forever.*

The psalm condenses Israel's history in terms of God's gifts to them: creation, deliverance, guidance, military victories, even food. And capping it all off—His faithful, never-ending love.

True gratitude, however, shares instead of hoarding—both the material and the spiritual. Lately, this question has been convicting me: Did God give us many gifts for our increased comfort or for displaying His love when we pass along those gifts to others?

The bottom line is gratitude. So we can pray,

> Oh, Ever-giving Lord,
> in our self-focused humanity,
> we sometimes forget to simply give You thanks
> for all the precious gifts You lavish on us.
> So please help us express our gratitude often—
> both in words
> and in sharing.

Journal Prompts

1. What came to your mind as you read today's devotion? Make notes or start writing a psalm about it. You may find it helpful to reread the following two paragraphs (from above) and pick at least one of the topics listed here (or one of your own) to write about:
    - "He has made us His children, His heirs along with Jesus, members of His family."
    - "He has given us His forgiveness, His Holy Spirit, His grace, His unfailing love, the precious assurance that He will never leave us.
    - He has given us His inexplicable peace and His all-sufficient strength to get us through anything. He has given us His promise that we'll be with our Savior the moment we say goodbye to this world."
2. Try writing a psalm in the format of Psalm 136:

- *Give thanks to*_____ (name or attribute of God)
- reason(s) for the praise (optional)
- followed by either *His faithful love endures forever* or another phrase that touches your heart.

There's an old prayer that goes something like this: "O God, you have given me so much. I ask for one more thing: a grateful heart."[51]
—Ron Klug

Omni-thanks

I give thanks to my omnipresent God,
always present with me
at the same time present with my loved ones,
for He is a God of unfailing love.
I give thanks to my omnipotent God,
nothing too difficult,
no impossibilities for Him,
for He is a God of unfailing love.
I give thanks to my omniscient God,
nothing He cannot understand,
no action or thought unwise,
for He is a God of unfailing love.
—Joyce K. Ellis

JOYCE K. ELLIS

The Most Damage
A confession psalm

Dear Adonai, my Lord, my Master,
When I first thought about writing to You about sin,
I wanted to find some way to use eloquent and poetic words.
The truth told, sin is neither of those.
Sin is the thing that does the most damage,
that preoccupies my thoughts day to day.
Even though You have given me knowledge and precepts
to protect against sin,
still the wisdom to refrain from it eludes me.
In my heart I often act out of jealousy, dishonesty,
and a desire to discredit others.
Too many other sins slip my awareness
because I refuse to acknowledge they exist
until even lies begin to seem truthful.
Please, Lord, do not give me what I deserve.
But rather care for me as a Father
who tirelessly guides and protects an unruly, fragile child,
one who does not know the hurt
caused by actions and words.
Guide me so that repetitive sins are no longer a habit,
and give me the gift of discernment.
Teach me to acknowledge You.
Your strength is the one chance I have at correcting myself.
Forgive me, allow reconciliation—
by Your grace alone I am forgiven,
no longer left alone to work through these issues.

OUR HEART PSALMS

You alone bring truth, love, and purity.
Look into my heart and cleanse it,
but also see the true depth of my love for You.
Bring me relief from myself,
settle me with peace,
ground me with Your Word and Truth.
My love always …
—Kim Shackelford

We do not pray to tell God what he does not know, nor to remind him of things he has forgotten. He already cares for the things we pray about; his attention to them has never flagged from the beginning, and his understanding is unfathomable. He has simply been waiting for us to care about them with him.[52]

—Tim Stafford

21

FEELING MY SIN

*How can I know all the sins lurking
in my heart?
Cleanse me from these hidden faults.
Keep your servant from deliberate sins!
Don't let them control me.
Then I will be free of guilt
and innocent of great sin!*
—Psalm 19:12–13

I knelt before a rocking chair in my living room, hurting terribly. Not a physical pain but a spiritual one. I couldn't quit sobbing—my worst-ever pain over my own sin. I won't detail the situation here in order to protect others. Suffice it to say that God had put His finger on a sin in my life, and the wound drilled deep. (You'll find a resulting confession psalm at the end of this devotion.) I hope I never have to go through such profound anguish again.

When God points out something in our lives that breaks His heart, we have two choices: we can ignore His prompting to deal with it, or we can confess that sin and vow that, by His grace, we won't "go there again." Unfortunately, the more we choose the ignore option, the more deaf we become to His voice—which lets us know when we've strayed—and the less God is inclined to listen to us. *If I had not confessed the sin in my heart, the Lord would not have listened* (Psalm 66:18).

But perhaps one reason we find ourselves repeating a past sin may be that we haven't identified the roots of that sin.

Many years ago, I heard a story of a young believer who stood to pray at his church's prayer meeting and pleaded, "Dear Lord, clean out the cobwebs of our lives." It seemed an appropriate prayer (and an effective metaphor, by the way). But week after week, without fail, he repeated the request: "Dear Lord, clean out the cobwebs our lives." Some people in the congregation joked privately about it, but no one dared say anything to the young man.

Finally, after several months and yet another "Dear Lord, clean out the cobwebs our lives," one of the elders of the church quickly jumped to his feet and shouted, "Oh, Lord! Forget the cobwebs. Kill the spider!"

Isn't it true that sometimes we become more preoccupied with sin's *evidence* than the hidden *causes*?

- We may confess a sharp word to a neighbor but be blind to our lack of love.
- We may confess that we covet a friend's new car but ignore our discontent with what God has provided for us.
- We may confess our worry but disregard our prideful thoughts that the solution is up to us.

Aren't pride and a weak faith in God hiding beneath many of our sins?

Writing psalms can be a way to explore the deep, hidden sins God already knows about but that we deny or rationalize. Maybe we don't even want to look for them. Yet intimacy with our holy God demands honest self-scrutiny.

Roger C. Palms writes, "There is sin, there is guilt, and we are loaded with both. Denying this is like denying the diagnosis of cancer—it is still there. Shutting our eyes won't make it go away." [53]

Two powerful truths dominate confession psalms:

1. God is holy.
2. Sin is real.

And sin causes real pain, real devastation. While psychologists from a secular worldview often dispense euphemisms to nullify responsibility, the Word of God clearly teaches that *the wages of sin is death* (Romans 6:23)—death to relationships, death to health, death to joy, death to a vital relationship with God.

Painful death.

That's why confession and restoration are so important.

And ever since the garden of Eden, God has been telling us He wants honesty, not cover-ups. The transaction is amazing: We confess our sins (admit that what we did was wrong). Then God, in His faithfulness and justice, forgives us because of what Jesus did for us on the cross (see 1 John 1:9). So we can pray,

> Oh, Lord of Truth,
> I know how sneaky self-deception can be
> and how easy it is to sin against others
> without even knowing it.
> (How devastating when we discover it!)
> So please increase my sensitivity.
> Help me see my sin for what it is,
> come to you for cleansing,
> and experience your loving forgiveness.

Journal Prompts

If the topic of confession makes you uncomfortable, reread the Tim Stafford quotation at the beginning of this devotion. Confession is difficult sometimes. We may feel like a child caught with a hand in the cookie jar—face red, cheeks burning, heart pounding.

But neglecting to confess our sins is one of the biggest hindrances to intimacy with our Creator, who loves us infinitely and wants to hold us close. If God has brought a particular sin to your mind, write about it on the lines below. You may want to write in a vague way, especially if the particulars could hurt others. Confess to God privately, in your heart, as much detail as you need to pour out. Then write down only what you would feel comfortable sharing with others. See my example below, using a common pattern for confession psalms in Scripture.

Writing out prayers of confession helps us hold still long enough to think and care about what God cares about—our sins and what they do to our relationship with Him and with others.

Elements for confession psalms
- cry for mercy
- call sin sin (specificity)

- admit our sin nature
- acknowledge God's holiness
- repent
- seek cleansing and restored relationship
- profess confidence in God
- promise God our praise

OUR HEART PSALMS

Confession Agony

Oh, my Holy God,
how grateful I am that in Your holiness
You also demonstrate Your mercy and grace,
and that's what I desperately need today!
Mercy to choose not to give me what I deserve—
Your condemnation.
Grace to give me what I don't deserve—Your pardon.
I'm kneeling before this rocking chair,
my arms leaning in and rocking back and forth,
back and forth,
sobbing over this sin I confess today.
And I feel Your heart break within my own heart.
This is not what You want for me.
Scour my heart clean, my God.
May the pain be the cure.
I claim the forgiveness You offer,
paid for by the pain Jesus suffered for my cure.
Restore my relationship with You
and rebuild my confidence to go on.
Hold me close,
reignite my joy,
and I will praise You again and again!
—Joyce K. Ellis

Tug-of-War
A confession psalm

Sovereign and Holy God,
how do You put up with me?
I don't deserve Your mercy but crave it desperately.
To me even the words "God, have mercy on me a sinner"
hang in the air with hollow arrogance.
This epidemic of pride within my heart—
this sin that repels and repulses You—
has permeated human DNA from Eden onward.
But I am without excuse.
My choices indict me.
I know You're in control, yet our tug-of-war
leaves rope burns, blisters of guilt.
The struggle is too painful, the futility too glaring.
King of my life, forgive once more,
reign once more,
for You rule much better than I.
And as Your humility replaces my pride,
I eagerly give You praise.
—Joyce K. Ellis

I ... am painfully aware that intimacy with God comes only when I am brutally honest with the Lord about specific sins in my life. I start making headway when I give up self-deception and stop playing games with myself and the Lord. Reality, not rationalization, leads to growth.[54]
—Don Wyrtzen

22

FEELING REMORSEFUL

My sins are staring me down.
—Psalm 51:3 (MSG)

Writing this book, in its various forms, has taken more than two decades, leaving scores of editor rejections in its wake. But as I started completely overhauling the material, I felt as if I were under full-frontal attack, as if the bottom fell out of my world and pulled me in after it.

In the middle of writing new chapters, I discovered that years earlier I had unknowingly, deeply wounded someone I love very much. Devastating consequences resulted. With a broken heart, I asked for and received forgiveness from God and from the precious one I hurt. But repercussions remain. I can't hit Control Z for an Undo like I can on my computer keyboard.

As I dealt with the pain, pride clawed its way into my self-examination. Which was worse? I wondered. The hurt I caused or the pride I had to confess to God, wondering how I could have been so blind? Sins of omission (things we knew we should do and didn't do) can create wounds as deep as sins of commission (things we did do). I'm still working through all this with the Lord.

But what is this hierarchy of sins we construct in our minds? Lying isn't as bad as stealing, perhaps? Swearing isn't as bad as murder but is worse than greed? Is greed worse than pride? Is pride the least offensive to God?

Where did we get this kind of thinking? Not Scripture. The Ten Commandments are not God's Top Ten List of Sins in descending order of severity.

Certainly, the penalty for homicide in a court of law is greater than that for perjury, but in God's eyes sin is sin. And every sin I commit is a slap in the face of our holy God—not to mention its destructive consequences within me and those I hurt.

C. S. Lewis called pride "the complete anti-God state of mind."[55] Think of that!

Pride enticed Lucifer (Satan's name before God kicked this prideful angel out of heaven) to challenge God for top billing in the heavenly realms. Then, masquerading as the friendly neighborhood serpent, he incited pride within Eve—a desire to be equal with God, the one in the know, the one in control.

When we come right down to it, every sin can be traced back to pride, can't it?

- Idolatry? Putting *me* (or *"my_____"*) before God.
- Adultery? Putting *my desires* before my commitment to my spouse.
- Lies? Putting the desire to "save *my* skin" before the truth.
- Murder? Putting *my* desire for revenge before God's sole right to vengeance.

And then, inevitably, *remorse* crashes down around any of us who want to please God and have an intimate relationship with Him.

The Psalms show us three responses to the realization of sin:

1. admission of no guilt: I'm suffering through no fault of my own (Psalm 109:1–5).
2. admission of limited guilt: I bear some responsibility for this painful situation, but it's not *all* my fault.
   Or I *have* sinned, but my enemies make it worse by gloating over my downfall (Psalm 38:17–19).
3. admission of total guilt: I'm in agony because of my own sin (Psalm 51).

This third category can motivate the deepest, most honest confession psalms.

Guilt comes for a reason, writes Walter Brueggemann. "Guilt can be destructive ... But guilt fully embraced and acknowledged permits movement, a new reception of life, and a new communion with God."[56] So we can pray,

> Oh, Holy God,
> remorse can debilitate,
> but we thank You that Jesus took all our sins
> on Himself to restore us to You and to one another.
> So please, by Your grace,
> restore our joy and strength
> in the process of forgiveness.

Journal Prompts

1. While you were reading this devotion, did God bring something to mind that you need to confess to Him? Make notes here and/or begin writing a confession psalm, seeking restoration with the Lord.
2. Sometimes we may want to write a confession psalm for a group we're in. (See the "psalms" written by Dietrich Bonhoeffer and Pastor Joe Wright below.)

You can use the following biblical pattern for a confession psalm (based on Psalm 51) for either kind of psalm:
- cry for mercy
- call sin sin (specificity)
- admit our sin nature
- acknowledge God's holiness
- repent
- seek cleansing and restored relationship
- profess confidence in God
- promise God our praise

OUR HEART PSALMS

JOYCE K. ELLIS

This excerpt from Dietrich Bonhoeffer is a cautionary "confession psalm" written during World War II on behalf of the church in Germany—apathetically blinded to Hitler's rise to power.

> Shrinking from pain and poor in deed,
> we have betrayed Thee before men.
> > Though we saw lies raise their head,
> > we dishonored the truth instead.
> > We saw brothers dying while we had breath
> > and feared only our own death.
> We come before Thee as men,
> confessing our sins.[57]

Self-Deception Confessed

"Confession psalm" written and delivered by Pastor Joe Wright, Central Christian Church, Wichita, Kansas, on the occasion of serving as guest chaplain for the Kansas House of Representatives, January 23, 1996.

Heavenly Father, we come before you today
to ask your forgiveness,
and to seek your direction and guidance.
We know your Word says, "Woe to those who call evil good,"
but that's exactly what we have done.
We have lost our spiritual equilibrium
and inverted our values.
We confess that we ridiculed the absolute truth of your Word
and called it moral pluralism.
We have worshipped other gods
and called it multi-culturalism.
We endorsed perversion and called it an alternative lifestyle.
We have exploited the poor and called it the lottery.
We have neglected the needy and called it self-preservation.
We have rewarded laziness and called it welfare ...
We've neglected to discipline our children
and called it building esteem ...
We have polluted the air with profanity and pornography
and called it freedom of expression ...
Search us, oh, God and know our hearts today;
try us and see if there be some wicked way in us;
cleanse us from every sin and set us free.[58]

God has promised to forgive us when we confess our sins (1 John 1:9). To doubt His forgiveness is to doubt His integrity. We are forgiven because He declared it, not because we feel it. We have no reason to let unbelief block the joy and peace and freedom that we have every right to experience.[59]
— David C. Egner

23

FEELING UNFORGIVEN[60]

*His unfailing love toward those who fear him
is as great as the height of the heavens above the earth.
He has removed our sins as far from us
as the east is from the west.*
—Psalm 103:11–12

I've always loved legal wrangling. In my childhood, our family watched TV shows such as *Perry Mason*, and I learned courtroom-battle terminology. District attorney Hamilton Burger frequently shot to his feet and objected to Perry's questions on the grounds that they were "incompetent, irrelevant, and immaterial."

Unlike many people, I've jumped at my two opportunities for jury duty. And as foreperson, I've read the verdict for my fellow jurors. The tension of a courtroom battle and the struggle for justice have helped equip me for spiritual battles.

It seemed insignificant at the time, and I was only a child. But I took something that didn't belong to me, knowing it was wrong. The details aren't important. I've waged this type of battle with other sins as well.

At first, I tried to rationalize the theft. But I had already committed my life to Jesus. So I became angry that I had given in to temptation. With God's prompting, I confessed my sin and claimed His promise that He is *faithful and just to forgive us our sins* (1 John 1:9).

Soon I became aware of the legal wrangling in the heavenly realms—and it intensified. Over and over, my thoughts returned to what I did. How could I, a believer—even a child-believer well taught in the Scriptures, do such a thing? Circumstances prevented restitution, but I asked God repeatedly to forgive me and erase the painful memory.

The guilt haunted me into my adulthood and resurfaced often as I tried to follow the Lord's calling on my life. The Enemy, like a prosecuting attorney, accused me of being "incompetent" to serve God. The battle raged on.

Then one day, a courtroom phrase came to mind. Sometimes, when an attorney questions a witness and receives an answer, the attorney will come at the same question from another angle, trying to trip up the witness. At that point, the opposing counsel may jump up and say, "I object, Your Honor. Asked and answered."

That was it—my answer for Satan, our "accuser" (Revelation 12:10).

I determined to listen no longer to the Enemy's accusations.

The Bible says we all sin. We all have actions or thoughts in our past—maybe in our present, too—that the Enemy uses to accuse us and make us feel—even believe—we are "incompetent, irrelevant, and immaterial."

But *we have an advocate [a defense attorney] who pleads our case before the Father,* the apostle John reminds us. *He is Jesus Christ, the one who is truly righteous. He himself is the sacrifice that atones for our sins—and not only our sins but the sins of all the world* (1 John 2:1–2, brackets added).

If we have accepted His payment for all our sins, we can say, on the authority of God's Word that *He has removed our sins as far from us as the east is from the west* (Psalm 103:12).

So every time the Enemy accuses me of wrongdoing in the courts of heaven, Jesus advocates on my behalf and gives me the authority to say, "I object! Asked and answered."

Gayle Roper writes about the great wedge the Enemy's accusations drive between us and our loving heavenly Father: "Satan's accusations cripple us and make us pull away from God in needless remorse and regret. In contrast, genuine Spirit-sent guilt turns us to God in repentance, to restore the damaged relationship between Parent and child. Once confession has been made, Spirit-induced guilt disappears, its purpose accomplished. If guilt continues beyond confession, it is not of God."[61]

Isn't that last sentence powerful?

So what, exactly, is confession? Pastor and writer David Daniels says that "to confess means to admit or concede. It involves stripping away layers of disguise to expose what is really at the center of who we are. Confession is the discipline of making an honest appraisal of ourselves."[62]

When we need to confess something to God, writing a confession psalm is a good way to nail down the fact that we have brought that sin to God, agreed with Him that it was wrong, and instantly received His forgiveness. (See a pattern below for confession psalms.)

Caution: an unhealthy preoccupation with sin can paralyze us. Could we even remember all our sins to confess them? David Daniels offers a comforting answer: "According to His compassion and mercy, God causes us to forget some of the sinful things we do ... We cannot confess every sin we've done, but we should confess any sin we remember. It's part of being completely honest with God."[63]

Sometimes a past sin comes to mind, and I can't remember if I confessed it to God. But if I have written a confession psalm in my journal about it, I know the date and time He forgave me. I can tell my mind to quiet down with "asked and answered." So we can pray,

> Oh, Holy and Just God,
> You are so precious,
> but sin is so ugly
> with such far-reaching, life-choking tentacles,
> so self-destructive, so painful.
> So ... please prompt me to confess my sin quickly,
> quit doing it,
> claim Your promised forgiveness,
> and silence the Accuser.

Journal Prompts

The ghosts of sins past have a way of haunting the present. The Enemy knows our vulnerability. He dangles the same temptations in front of us time after time—even some we thought we had conquered.

Sit quietly for a few minutes, and listen for God's voice. Ask Him to show you anything that's standing in the way of a more intimate relationship with Him. Probe your memory. Make note of any thoughts He brings to mind. Confess that sin—Jesus died to forgive it—and accept God's forgiveness. If words come, begin writing a confession psalm to nail down the day You received His forgiveness. And find restoration in His loving arms.

_____

_____

_____

_____

_____

_____

_____

_____

_____

_____

_____

_____

OUR HEART PSALMS

No Excuses
A confession psalm

I stand beside my Advocate in God's courtroom
as the charge is read.
"How do you plead?" the Righteous Judge cries out.
I hang my head.
No arguing.
No rationalization.
No excuses.
"Guilty as charged, Your Honor," I whisper.
The Righteous Judge eyes my Advocate,
the agony apparent.
The gavel bangs.
"Forgiven," he cries. "Case dismissed."
—Joyce K. Ellis

Forgiveness

Lord, I thank you for the joy of forgiveness.
I remember the surprise of it.
My guilt was like low-level chronic pain.
When it was removed, I realized
it had drained my life of joy and confidence.
Let me remember my forgiveness
so that I have a light heart
that is quick to enjoy life and other people. Amen.[64]

—Timothy and Kathy Keller
(adaptation to a poetic psalm style, mine)

Even if we have made unwise choices, bypassed opportunities, or sinned miserably, it is not too late to begin to do what God wants us to do![65]
—Erwin W. Lutzer

24
FEELING LIKE A FAILURE

*Though they stumble, they will never fall,
for the Lord holds them by the hand.*
—Psalm 37:24

During my freshman year in high school, I began studying Spanish. My interest piqued, I think, with my grandparents' involvement in a Spanish literature outreach. And when I was a little girl, I felt the Lord had called me to be a missionary—probably to Latin America. I had to excel at learning the language.

A couple of weeks after my high school graduation, I traveled—alone, at the age of seventeen—to Central America, to work with a missionary family there.

Though independent for my age, I soon felt overwhelmed with the culture shock, homesickness, and differences between classroom Spanish and lightning-fast, real-world Spanish. My favorite phrase became *"Más despacio, por favor"* (slower, please). And the missionary family didn't allow me to speak any English for the three months I lived with them—another layer to the challenges.

I made many vocabulary mistakes. One day I was shopping in the market with the conservative missionary woman, and I saw some luscious, ripe cherries (*cerezas*, in Spanish). *"Me encanta cervezas,"* I said. (I love beers.) Oops! Wrong word. What a boozer I must have seemed to the woman selling cerezas. And how embarrassing for my missionary hostess!

Though I loved my opportunities for serving Christ there, I came home from that trip feeling like a failure. All the dreams of the way my life would unfold evaporated.

Over the years, the Lord had to redefine the term *missionary* for me, but He has opened doors of cross-cultural ministry I never dreamed possible—both here and in Central America. Now I'm studying Spanish again, via Skype, for yearly short-term mission trips.

The problem is that I'm a perfectionist—in some areas. And learning Spanish is one of those areas. I do my homework each week, certain all my answers are correct, but after my lesson, my notebook bleeds with self-inflicted, red-ink corrections. Sometimes I feel like I'm in a pass/fail class—and

I'm not passing. In fact, I've forgotten grammar points and vocabulary I thought I had learned months ago.

While language mistakes may seem like minor failures, I've also had more serious failures, unmet expectations, unreached goals, and unfulfilled desires to please my Savior. They seem to spiral downward:

- I made a mistake/fell short of a goal (or a number of them).
- I failed (more intensity).
- I am a failure (cumulative effect defining who I am).

What happens when we pour time and money into a project we believe in—but it bombs?

What happens when we pour our lives into people we're mentoring—but they stab us in the back?

What happens when we pour our energy into living for Christ—but, in a moment of weakness, we sin and jeopardize future ministry for Christ?

Feelings of failure—whatever the situation—can be devastating, especially when we feel we've let *others* down or wounded them.

We undoubtedly wonder where we went wrong. And in the arena of parenting, we may begin to wonder if we ever did anything *right*. We may beat ourselves up over our failures so much that we erect a roadblock between us and what the Lord still wants to do in and through us. Dr. Erwin Lutzer, pastor and radio broadcaster, writes, "We forget that God is a specialist. He is well able to work our failures into His plans."[66]

How? Reread the verse at the beginning of this devotion: *Though they stumble, they will never fall, for the Lord holds them by the hand* (Psalm 37:24). As I thought about this verse one day, it reminded me of the lyrics of an old gospel song, "Precious Lord, Take My Hand."

An image came to mind—an image of me, with failure feelings written all over my face. I cry out to the Lord and reach up for His hand. When I do, I see the scar from that painful spike in Jesus' hand. He wraps it lovingly around my own. I feel the wound. And tears fill my eyes. Intimate relationship! He understands.

Once again, we develop a deeper intimacy with our Loving Creator when we honestly pour out our feelings of inadequacy, failure, and embarrassment. When we give up our self-battering habit, our Savior can comfort us and redeem the situation. But we need time alone with Him—time to gain perspective. These situations are setbacks, not failures.

Charles Swindoll says that "the best things we learn from mistakes [failures] are learned in secret, for it is there He [God] tells us His secrets, and in doing so, covers us with His love and understanding" [brackets mine].[67] So we can pray,

> Oh, Precious Redeemer,
> we know all too well our frailties, faults, and failures.
> They're so self-destructive.
> So please help us to quit beating ourselves up over them.
> Help us confess what needs to be confessed,
> forsake what needs to be forsaken,
> and accept what needs to be accepted—
> especially Your loving, understanding, nail-scarred hand
> of unfailing love and comfort.
> And help us keep moving forward with—and for—You.

Journal Prompts

Write about a time you failed or made a horribly embarrassing mistake. Have you ever felt like you were a complete failure? How did your thought processes move from "I made a mistake" to "I am a failure"? Has God helped you put the situation into perspective yet? Write a psalm of confession, thanksgiving, confidence, or wisdom. Use the patterns in the appendix if you find them useful.

OUR HEART PSALMS

> God does not want [us]
> to praise Him only when [we] are on the mountaintop
> surveying Canaan, the promised land.
> God desires much more to see His people writing psalms
> and praising Him when [we]
> "walk through the valley of the shadow of death."
> This is genuine praise.[68]
>
> —Watchman Nee
> (poetic arrangement mine)

OUR HEART PSALMS

Sometimes God is most present
when our suffering can make Him seem most absent.
Sometimes when we are in the fog and are unable to see
much on our own,
we need people by our side to show us where they see God
in our lives.
Sometimes we mistake God's respectfulness
for absence.
Understandably there are times when we want God to be
more obvious.
But God desires to reveal Himself clearly to those who
desire Him,
without revealing Himself forcibly to those who do not.
He wants us to follow Him not because He is overpowering,
but because we trust Him.[69]

—Ravi Zacharias and Vince Vitale
(poetic arrangement mine)

Nothing brings greater hope in the Christian faith than the fact that the relationship God desires with each one of us is not fleeting or for a limited time only. Because Jesus endured suffering to the end, and yet by His resurrection proved that death is not the end, our friendship with God can be for all eternity.[70]

—Ravi Zacharias and Vince Vitale

25

FEELING HOPEFUL

*When doubts filled my mind,
your comfort gave me renewed hope and cheer.*
—Psalm 94:19

A few years before my father died with Alzheimer's disease, he fell and broke his leg just below the hip. As I waited with him for surgery the next morning, every few minutes a cruel muscle spasm tugged at his fracture. With each new spasm, he threw back his head, raised his good knee, and, with a wild look in his eyes, screamed so loud I was sure he could be heard all the way down the hospital corridor. The prescribed morphine didn't help much.

My eyes filled with tears, watching him. I couldn't imagine what his pain felt like. Often he couldn't remember why he was in so much agony. He didn't remember his fall. I struggled for some way to comfort him. I stroked his hand. I repeated over and over what was causing the pain and told him about the impending surgery.

Having read the Shepherd Psalm that morning, I asked, "Dad, can you remember the twenty-third psalm?" Some of Dad's older memory-bank deposits still tumbled out when prompted—though comments made a moment earlier had already escaped.

He responded with a faraway look, so I primed the pump: *"The Lord is my shepherd ..."*

"I ... shall ... not ... want." His slurred, confused speech strung together the words of the King James Version he had memorized decades before. For a little while, he grew calmer, the comfort of his Shepherd at work.

Together we recited a few more lines. Then another wave of pain hit, and a nurse arrived with more morphine. We didn't get much further before he fell into a fitful sleep. But I believe God's peaceful assurance from that psalm helped us both endure those scary hours.

In times like these, when God helps us put our hope in Him, how fitting it is to praise Him. From deep down in our soul, we can express that confidence in a psalm.

In some ways, we might think of a confidence psalm as the *opposite* of a lament—at least the first part of a lament. The writer has processed the pain and emerged with a stronger faith. But the emotions and tones are so different that we can scarcely imagine that the same person wrote these laments and confidence psalms.

> **Lament** says, "I can't take any more!"
> **Confidence** says, "You, Lord, can take me through anything!"
> **Lament** says, "I'm scared to death."
> **Confidence** says, "I fear no evil."
> **Lament** says, "God, You've abandoned me!"
> **Confidence** says, "I know You're always with me even when I can't see or feel You."

What makes the difference?
- The passage of time?
- Recalling God's deliverance in the past?
- A seasoned, maturing relationship with our Savior?
- All of the above?

Perhaps the greatest difference is perspective—where we look.

In Psalm 121, another classic confidence psalm, the writer looks toward the distant mountains around Jerusalem and says, *Where will my help come from?*

My help comes from the Lord, the Maker of heaven and earth (vv. 1–2 HCSB).

We take our eyes off ourselves and our problems and look up. We rivet our eyes on our Creator, the One in control. That's the foundation for a psalm of trust, of confidence, of hope that can sustain us and blanket the fearful situation with peace. And when we write down our confidence psalms, they nurture our faith—and the faith of others, if we don't keep them a secret. So we can pray,

> Oh, Faithful God, we affirm our hope in You.
> You are our Shepherd,
> Your Word comforts us and gives us hope.
> So please help us keep coming to You.
> We dare not put our confidence anywhere else.

Journal Prompts

Write about a time when the Lord gave you a hope that buoyed you up through a difficult time. Or write about a time you faced a fearful situation and walked boldly ahead, confident in God. Or begin with a call to trust, such as "Come praise the Lord with me."

What would you like to shout from the rooftops about your great God? In our age of multiculturalism, what makes our God the only One to trust—as opposed to one of many gods in the all-roads-lead-to-God/heaven philosophy? Write about it.

OUR HEART PSALMS

What's in a confidence psalm?

Though the patterns of confidence psalms aren't as easily defined as other categories of psalms, confidence psalms often contain the following:

- affirmation of trust or assertion of the trustworthiness of God
- reasons for confidence (who God is, what He does, benefits of trust)
- reality of crisis or cause of fear
- assurance of God's presence
- promise of future help/eternal hope

Some confidence psalms, like the one on the next page by Pat Jaakkola, pour out during times of peace. Notice how many of the above elements she employed. Her expression of trust and praise resonates with the joyful heart.

Overwhelming Joy
A confidence psalm

Today I felt overwhelmed with the love of God,
so filled with His Spirit.
It felt good,
the confidence that nothing could take His love away,
to be accepted as I am, not judged for what I am not,
to know that there is much that needs to be changed in me
and that He doesn't give up on me.
He won't leave me where I am.
What inner joy comes from knowing the Lord.
Thank You, Father, for a joy that can't be explained, just felt.
Let my joy in You spill over to others.
—Pat Jaakkola

Enthronement Psalms

Enthronement psalms (also called royal psalms) are a category that exalts God as the king on the throne, ruling over all humanity and creation.

The psalm below employs another common technique used in many psalms, something I call bookending—a repetition of the opening words of praise to conclude the psalm—for emphasis. This is another element you may want to include in your psalms.

Praise to the Lord who reigns in holiness
Praise to our God who reigns in power
Praise our Redeemer in whom love and justice meet
Praise our great King on the throne.

Holy, Almighty,
Unfailing love is He
Always a just God
He reigns eternally

Praise to the Lord who reigns in holiness
Praise to our God who reigns in power
Praise our Redeemer in whom love and justice meet
Praise our great King on the throne.
—Joyce K. Ellis

III

TIMELY, TIMELESS PRAISE

When we relax in the arms of our Good Shepherd in Psalm 23, confess our sin along with David in Psalm 51, or let our spirits soar on a star-spangled night with praise to the Creator of all that glory in Psalm 19, we suspend time, in a sense.

We identify with countless believers over the centuries who have done the same. We join a time warp of tribute to the Great God and Father of our Lord Jesus Christ, for whom no amount of praise is too much.

> *You have made us for Yourself,*
> *and our hearts are restless*
> *until they rest in You.*[71]
> —Augustine of Hippo

Shyness, beauty, eloquence, race, sophistication—none of these matter, only loyalty to the Head [of the Body, the Lord Jesus Christ], and through the Head to each other.[72]

—Dr. Paul Brand and Philip Yancey
(brackets added)

26

ACCEPTING THE WAY GOD MADE ME

*You made all the delicate, inner
parts of my body
and knit me together in my mother's womb.
Thank you for making me so
wonderfully complex!
Your workmanship is marvelous—how
well I know it.
You watched me as I was being formed
in utter seclusion,
as I was woven together in the dark
of the womb.
You saw me before I was born.
Every day of my life was recorded in
your book.
Every moment was laid out
before a single day had passed.*
—Psalm 139:13–16

For a brief period when I was very young, I wanted to be a movie or TV star. Alone in the privacy of my bedroom, I sat in front of my dresser mirror, held up a bottle of shampoo or other favorite item, and pretended I was looking into a TV camera, "selling" that product with all the charm I could muster. From there it was only a short hop to feature films, right?

But those dreams quickly faded because I felt I wasn't pretty enough, skinny enough, or talented enough. I hadn't considered the successful frumpy "Aunt Bees" of television fame (*The Andy Griffith Show*) or the pointy-nosed Phyllis Dillers of the comedic entertainment world. Nor had I analyzed the criteria by which I was measuring beauty and talent. In time, the Lord redirected my desires and aspirations.

A few years ago, while visiting with a young teenager, I asked her what she wanted to do with her life. "I want to be famous," she said. "I don't care what for. I just want to be famous." Someday she may discover a common obstacle to gaining even the proverbial fifteen minutes of fame: she's not _____ enough.

Biographies of famous people, including successful actors, often reveal huge insecurities. One actor admitted that every day he showed up at the set he was afraid people would find out he wasn't as good as they thought, and he would be fired.

Not _____ enough. How we fill in that blank tells us a lot about how we see ourselves.

Men and women spend billions each year, trying to become attractive enough, skinny enough, valuable enough—as a potential spouse, new hire, or someone they themselves can stand to look at in the mirror.

A good self-image has become a "god" for many.

What's most important, however, is not the way we see ourselves or others see us but the way God sees us. When we truly take to heart the words of Psalm 139 (at the beginning of this devotion), we can gain more confidence about our "enough."

Our Beyond-Genius God, lovingly and personally (according to the psalm) wove together every molecule of our bodies—each organ, each muscle, each bone. Every cell, every DNA particle that dictated our hair and eye color, our body type, our skin tone, and our fingerprints. He took the same care in the creative process for every other human being He released into our world.

Imagine that! If He took that much care in creating us, consider our incredible inherent worth to Him. Whether or not we feel it. Whether or not others see it.

The apostle John, in his account of the life of Christ, refers to himself as the disciple Jesus loved.

And his writing reflects his overwhelming sense of God's love that made possible their intimate relationship. John wrote: *Look at how great a love the Father has given us that we should be called God's children. And we are!* (1 John 3:1 HCSB).

Another version uses the phrase *lavished on us* instead of *given us*. What if we truly felt the lavish love of our Creator? What if that lavish love permeated our self-identity so much that we signed all our letters and emails "the disciple Jesus loves"?

Accepting the way God made us requires some caution, however. He gave us free will, and we cannot excuse any disobedience by saying, "That's just the way God made me." Our failure to obey what He has clearly laid out in His Word is our choice. And He longs for us to respond to His lavish love by doing what pleases Him.

The focus on self-acceptance, self-image, and self-worth also yields emptiness when we focus primarily on the "self" part. Without God's eternal perspective, we enter a vicious cycle: self-acceptance keeps needing to be pumped up ... we may feel important or accepted for a time ... pride takes over ... we mess up ... insecurities resurface ... we crash like a five-year-old after a sugar high ... and we have to start pumping up that self-acceptance again.

What's missing? Two key roles in our lives:
1. The perpetual role of our Creator: our "enough" is rooted in His all-sufficiency and the way He wants to shape us into His dream for us.
2. The essential role of others, especially spiritual mentors and other believers—not as a source to keep pumping us up but as those who can help us maintain an eternal perspective.

How extraordinarily freeing! Our confidence is in Him and His comprehensive plans for us. So we can pray,

> Oh, Loving Creator,
> how easily "self" barges in,
> getting in the way
> of realizing Your dreams for us.
> So please guard us against
> both self-centeredness and self-loathing
> and help us find our "enough"
> in Your amazing, lavish, intimate love.

Journal Prompts

What is the Lord teaching you about the way He sees you? About the way He wants you to see yourself? Make notes here and begin working these thoughts into a confidence psalm, proclaiming that your confidence comes from who you are *in Him*. (See elements of confidence psalms in the appendix.)

OUR HEART PSALMS

Oh, to have one's soul under heavenly cultivation;
no longer a wilderness,
but a garden of the Lord!
Enclosed from the waste, walled around by grace,
planted by instruction, visited by love,
weeded by heavenly discipline, and guarded by divine power,
one's favored soul is prepared to yield fruit unto the Lord.[73]
—Charles Spurgeon
(arrangement in poetic psalm style mine)

All-Sensing
A hymn psalm

The Lord's vision is pure.
He envisioned the colorful, soft and bold but fragile flowers
and the erect strength and grain of the mighty trees.
His sight observes the sinister and the innocent.
Yes, the Lord's eyes see all.
The Lord's hearing is perfect.
He is attentive as the songbirds call out
softly with sounds of joy, singing His glory.
His contemplation is full,
hearing the weak, whimpering prayer of a hurting soul.
Yes, the Lord's ears listen to all of creation.
The Lord's touch is priceless.
His powerful greatness displayed
in the rolling, shimmering waters of a great river.
His caring gentleness in the soft, flowing hair
of a young child.
Yes, the Lord's hand impacts all of creation on earth.
The Lord's vision is pure,
yes, the Lord's eyes see all.
The Lord's hearing is perfect,
yes, the Lord's ears listen to all of creation.
The Lord's touch is priceless,
yes, the Lord's hand impacts all of creation on earth.
—Kim Shackelford

Deepening intimacy with God is the outcome of deep desire. Only those who count such intimacy a prize worth sacrificing anything else for, are likely to attain it ... We are now, and we will be in the future, only as intimate with God as we really choose to be.[74]
—J. Oswald Sanders

27

INTIMACY WITH MY CREATOR

The Lord is near all who call out to Him,
all who call out to Him with integrity ...
let every living thing
praise His holy name forever and ever.
—Psalms 145:18, 21 (HCSB)

At age four, our middle child learned the folk song, "Kum Ba Ya," (which many people think of as "Come by Here").[75] In that little song, she found a gold mine. With one simple tune, she could plug in a few different words and have a new verse:

Someone's gettin' dressed, Lord
Someone's washin' their hair, Lord
Someone's goin' to the store, Lord
Someone's waitin', Lord
Someone's doin' sumpin', Lord.

And on and on she went, each time repeating the phrase the proper number of times and ending with "Oh, Lord, kum ba ya."

Mother tired more quickly of the song than daughter did (so much for the short attention span of preschoolers). On a kum ba ya, it seemed, a child could sing forever—or until Mom was kum-ba-yahed out.

But as I heard her understanding of the Lord's presence in our lives (Emmanuel—God with us), I marveled at her well-developed theology. All too often, little irritations and big crises overshadow our understanding of His continual, caring presence in our lives. And I smiled at her reminders that God was with me in the washing of my hair as much as in singing in the church choir. No wonder Jesus highly values childlike faith.

O Lord ... You know when I sit down or stand up ... David wrote. *You see me when I travel and when I rest at home. You know everything I do* (Psalm 139:1–3).

He is, indeed, intimately acquainted with all our ways, and I long to be intimately acquainted with all of His.

Our own self-concept is deeply rooted in our concept of God, so it's important to understand that connection. In Psalm 8, a hymn psalm, David marvels at the worth God places on every human being, rooted in the infinite worth of our Almighty, majestic Creator.

OUR HEART PSALMS

Through a hymn psalm, we can explore the depths of what we're learning about God and praise Him over and over for who He is.

A husband and wife get to know each other over months and years by spending time together, observing each other, being honest with each other, and seeking to please and honor each other. We grow in intimacy with God the same way. We learn what pleases Him, what dishonors Him, and what we can expect from Him.

One way our hearts can respond is to write a hymn psalm, which finds its roots in that deepening intimacy—that close encounter of a most personal kind. And our journey with God gives us so much to write about.

At times we can only pray, "I love you, Lord" (which would be a teeny praise psalm) or "Help, Lord!" (a wee lament psalm). But what a lovely gift of time and emotional investment we can give to God, and ourselves, by letting our thoughts and emotions disentangle themselves through our fingertips.

Rich psalms develop as we vulnerably express our feelings and make new connections between mind and heart. So we can pray,

Oh, Great yet Deeply Personal God,
we thank You that You long for an honest,
intimate relationship with us
and You love to hear us tell You how much we love You.
So please help us feel You drawing us close
to abandon our awkwardness
and freely express the love You've put in our hearts
for only You.

Journal Prompts

In the time you've been following God, what are you learning about His character? Which of His attributes are most meaningful to you at this point in your life? How have you experienced that characteristic of God? Make notes here, maybe including an anecdote, or go ahead and begin writing a hymn psalm. You may want to read that psalm to others to encourage them.

Patterns for hymn psalms can vary, but we can often boil them down to this:

> Call to praise
> Reasons for praise
> Further words of praise
> > often a repetition of the first call to praise, creating a bookend effect

OUR HEART PSALMS

Here's an example:

Psalm 103
(excerpt)

Let all that I am praise the Lord;
with my whole heart, I will praise his holy name.
Let all that I am praise the Lord;
may I never forget the good things he does for me.
He forgives all my sins
and heals all my diseases.
He redeems me from death
and crowns me with love and tender mercies.
He fills my life with good things.
My youth is renewed like the eagle's! …
Praise the Lord, everything he has created,
everything in all his kingdom.
Let all that I am praise the Lord.

_____

_____

_____

_____

_____

_____

_____

_____

_____

_____

OUR HEART PSALMS

Legacy
A wisdom psalm

Listen, children,
to seven things you need to know,
not the only seven things you need to know
but some of the more important,
wisdom seldom discussed in one sitting
but a truth legacy
vital to pass on:

Honesty with God is like breathing
clean mountain air,
but hiding your emotions from Him is like inhaling
secondhand smoke.

God's Word is not a litany of edicts
to prohibit fun on life's journey.
It's the road map for a more rewarding trip.

God's in charge. We're not.
There's no room for fear. Rest in that.

What's the point in wearing yourself out?
It's better to make room for relaxation
than forced bed rest.

Richer is the person with open hands
than the one with tight fists.

OUR HEART PSALMS

Accept God's unconditional love
without reservation.
Dispense God's unconditional love
like the loaves and fishes Jesus multiplied.

Nothing is less important than demanding your rights.
Nothing is more important than trusting God completely.
—Joyce K. Ellis

If sacrifice is indeed the ecstasy of giving the best we have to the one we love the most, it inevitably follows that there will often be simple, mundane rights as well that must be renounced for love of our Lord.[76]
—J. Oswald Sanders

28

A SACRIFICE OF PRAISE

I will sacrifice a voluntary offering to you;
I will praise your name, O Lord,
for it is good.
—Psalm 54:6

Disappointments. Failures. Unmet expectations. Financial crises. Interpersonal conflicts. Chronic health struggles. I have more than a nodding acquaintance with these kinds of challenges. I know how much they can overwhelm us—especially when they pile up, one after another. That's what it's been like while I've been writing this book. A friend recently told me it seems like I'm living a Joblike existence.

My challenges haven't been nearly as severe as Job's. But they do seem relentless sometimes. What has always touched me about Job's story is the pounding wave upon wave of disaster.

According to the historical account in Job chapter 1, this extremely wealthy yet godly man first learns from a messenger that a band of marauders attacked his servants in the field. The invaders killed all the servants (except the messenger who escaped to tell what happened) and made off with all Job's donkeys and oxen.

The next five words are key: *While he [the messenger] was still speaking* ... (v. 16). Messenger #2 shows up. I get the feeling he had been running a great distance and arrived, gasping for oxygen. He knows nothing of what the first news bearer had said. He simply blurts out what he saw: a huge fireball from the sky crashed into the fields and burned to death Job's thousands of sheep and all his shepherds. Again, only this messenger escaped to report the catastrophe.

Then come those five words again: *While he was still speaking* ... (v. 17). Messenger #3's breathless news: Not one, not two, but three groups of foreigners stole all Job's camels and slaughtered all the attending servants—except the messenger.

While Messenger #3 *was still speaking* (v. 18), messenger #4 comes with the worst news of all. Job's ten grown children were partying at one of their houses. Suddenly, a fierce, cyclone-type wind hit, destroying the house and killing every one of his offspring. Only this messenger survived to tell the story.

Imagine Job's crushing grief. Can you feel it? Have you been there? How could Job even breathe? He walks through his culture's grieving rituals. But, incredibly, his next move is to fall to the ground in worship. Worship!

Evidently, Job's was a living, well-worn faith—not a faith he grasped for in a crisis situation. He leaned on his well-established, intimate, honest relationship with his Creator. Job cried out, acknowledging that the Sovereign Lord had given Job everything he owned. And his Sovereign Lord had every right to take it away.

"Praise the name of the Lord!" he exclaims (v. 21). Job doesn't blame God. He praises Him. This isn't a quick, don't-worry-be-happy philosophy. He's not in denial. It's an acceptance born of intimacy with the God he loves.

It's not easy to praise God during tough times, but it's worth it. He's worth it.

God's Word reminds us that we're not earthbound people: This world is not our permanent home (Hebrews 13:14). This life isn't all there is. Therefore, verse 15 continues, *let us offer through Jesus a continual* **sacrifice of praise** *to God, proclaiming our allegiance to his name* (emphasis mine).

Sacrifice of praise? Yes, sometimes I feel like it's a sacrifice for me to praise God. I don't think I'm alone in that.

So what do we have to sacrifice—or give up—to focus on God and praise Him?

A lot. Possessiveness. Self-pity. Self-importance. Pride. Self-centeredness. Self-sufficiency. Maybe our whole vision of what our life is supposed to be like or what God has called us to do.

Often it's difficult to refocus our vision in the midst of calamity or disappointment. But once we get there, we'll enjoy the view. So we can pray,

> Oh, God of Comfort, we don't have to deny
> the pain of loss and disappointment.
> It hurts deeply, and we honestly admit that to You.
> But your prescription is to keep focusing on You.
> Praising You is our highest calling.
> So please help us to let go of our desire for control.
> Help us to acknowledge that everything we are and have
> is from Your loving hand,
> and help us to lift up to You
> a sacrifice of praise.

Journal Prompts

Maybe you're in a difficult place today, or a hurtful time from your past comes to mind. What may God be asking you to sacrifice in order to give Him the praise He deserves even in that situation?

What can you praise Him or thank Him for? In what ways has God shown His goodness and faithfulness to you, your family, your church, or your community? Jot down some ideas for a psalm. When you're ready, write a praise psalm to your loving Lord.

JOYCE K. ELLIS

You Were the One
A praise psalm

I called to You in the storms of my life.
I thought You didn't hear me, that You didn't care.
You were the one who held me up when I was falling.
You were the one who pulled me back when I strayed too far.
You were the one who listened when no one else would.
How can I ever praise You enough?
All that I am, all that I have, I owe to You—
to You be the glory.
I praise You, Father.
—Pat Jaakkola

True Freedom
A wisdom psalm

Sit still and consider the outcome of pain.
I called to the Lord in my entrapment
and He brought me one step closer to the defeat of my sin.
Sit still and ponder what He has done.
His sovereignty dealt a blow,
but His hands have also brought spiritual healing to my soul.
By His wounds, I am healed,
not necessarily of the pain,
but of the sin that so easily enslaves me.
This is true freedom!
Remember with Job: God, You can do all things,
and no purpose of Yours can be thwarted.
So I praise You for planning my pain
so that Your purpose of delivering me of my sin
could be done.
I thank You for loving me enough to afflict me
so I can be more intimate with You
as the shadows of my "sin traps" begin to dissipate.
—Delaine Gamache

Wisdom is the ability to look at life and its difficulties from God's point of view. As I learn more of the Word of God ... I see the world through the eyes of someone who is infinitely wise, entirely good, and whose agenda includes the wellbeing of all people ... [seeing] my circumstances as opportunities designed to develop me and train me as His vessel ... removes bitterness and irritation from my life and replaces them with gratitude and enthusiasm![77]
—Charles R. Swindoll

29

THE A TO Z OF PRAISE

*In the fear of the Lord one has strong confidence
and his children have a refuge.*
—Proverbs 14:26 (HCSB)

Just when you think your kids haven't heard a word you've said, they can surprise you. Though our three offspring are grown now, they frequently remind their dad and me of catchphrases or sayings we repeated over and over when they were younger.

One of my most memorable lines often popped out after they had disobeyed and then suffered repercussions of their own making. Parental punishment seemed like overkill, so I'd say, "Sometimes when we're naughty, we wind up punishing ourselves."

I suspect most families have repeated their own bits of wisdom over the years. And immortalizing them in a wisdom psalm can bring growth as well as enjoyment. For example, what have you discovered about the fear of the Lord, about obedience to His will, or about the character of God? What have you observed about the contrast between those who follow Him faithfully and those who have no use for their Creator?

For the first seven years of our marriage, my husband and I worked with a small inner-city church in downtown Minneapolis. The handful of volunteer leadership used cars and vans to bus in more than a hundred kids and adults from surrounding housing projects. All of us poured our lives into the children's programs, Bible studies, and other activities.

I had been raised in a traditional two-parent Christian family. So during that time in the inner city, I observed much about a world previously foreign to me. For instance, one day, as one of our colleagues was bringing a youngster home after an outing, he saw a man he'd never seen before leaving the house. "Is that your dad?" he asked the boy. "One of 'em," the boy replied.

Out of those years came new understandings and new questions, which I later turned into a wisdom psalm, called "Blessed Are They Who Mourn." (See the end of this devotion.)

When we've learned something from God that has jarred our thinking or behavior, we may want to climb on the nearest rooftop and shout out the truths we've learned to help others avoid the mistakes or heartaches we've endured.

Sometimes taking a step back to get an overview of what we've learned from God can provide perspective in our present challenges. And that perspective may help us guide our children or others who look to us for counsel. Don't underestimate the wisdom the Lord has *entrusted* to you. No matter where you are in your relationship with God, you undoubtedly have discovered important truths others have not yet learned.

Wisdom psalms frequently begin with a direct address to the reader. Examples: *Don't be stupid like a horse or a mule, which must be controlled with a bit and bridle to make it submit.* (Psalm 32:9 GNT). Or *Watch the blameless and observe the upright, for [because] ...* (Psalm 37:37 HCSB).

Other times they simply pass along observations: *Happy are those who reject the advice of evil people, who do not follow the example of sinners or join those who have no use for God. Instead, they find joy in obeying the Law of the Lord, and they study it day and night* (Psalm 1:1–2 GNT).

In essence, wisdom psalms feature proverbs within psalms. They are psalms that offer praise to God through wise insights. They may also contain promises for the believer to claim.

Through all the ups and downs of life, God teaches us important principles about getting along with people, lifestyle decisions, and pleasing Him. And we want to pass these on. That's what parents do. That's what teachers do. That's what many of us do by nature. We want to help others avoid our mistakes or benefit from the good consequences we've seen from submission to God. So we can pray,

> Oh, Sovereign Lord, I have much to learn,
> but You've also taught me so much,
> and I dare not be a truth hoarder.
> So please help me to be vulnerable,
> not only before You
> but before others
> so I don't waste the pain or challenges.

Journal Prompts

As I mentioned above, some passages in wisdom psalms sound like someone lifted them right out of the book of Proverbs. From the insights God has given us, we can write our own wisdom psalms, claiming God's promises and offering Him praise.

Suppose you are on your deathbed. One of your children or friends asks you what is the most important thing you've learned throughout your relationship with God. What would you say? How could you incorporate that into a wisdom psalm?

Think through some of the ups and downs in your faith journey. What are you learning from the pain and joy God has brought into your life?

Patterns

Wisdom psalms are identified more by tone or content than form, but Psalm 49 gives some helpful riverbanks:[78]

- summons to hear
- wisdom
- question
- question answered
- but (turning point—what I've called the Picardy Third)
- certainty of being heard

Motifs or Content
- blessing
- warning
- direct address to reader (e.g. *consider, observe*)

Blessed Are They Who Mourn
A wisdom psalm

Blessed are they who mourn
    for the children
        who wear a key around their neck.
Blessed are they who mourn
    for the single mother
        who must labor to provide for them ...
Blessed are they who mourn
    for the millions of children
        who die for lack of nourishment.
Blessed are they who mourn
    for those whose stomachs
        are never satisfied.
Blessed are they who mourn
    for the exhausted homemaker
        who doesn't know where
        her husband slept last night.
Blessed are they who mourn
    for the stressed-out husband
        with unfulfilled ambitions.
Blessed are they who mourn
    for those who hope someone will care.
Blessed are they who mourn
    for those beyond hoping.
True mourning is blending
our time and their problems—
        for those who become part of the solution
        shall understand the meaning of comfort.[79]
—Joyce K. Ellis

Remember
A wisdom psalm

Listen, all you who love the Lord:

Never forget that God is still in control.
Always remember that nothing is impossible for Him.
>   He is the ultimate victor!

Never forget that the Enemy is strong.
Always remember that God is infinitely stronger.
>   He will strengthen you for the battle.

Never forget that God is your Gentle Shepherd.
Always remember to give your worries to Him.
>   He wants to lighten your load.

Never forget that God is a God of joy.
Always remember to delight yourself in Him.
>   He wants His joy to shine through you to others.

Never forget that you are precious to God.
Always remember that He has plans for you.
>   His plans are always for your good and His glory.

Listen, all you who love the Lord:
God always was, is now, and always will be,
totally in control.
—Joyce K. Ellis

Acrostics

Word puzzles can be fun, and at least nine of the poems in the book of Psalms are acrostics built on the Hebrew alphabet.

For example, Psalm 119 consists of 22 stanzas of eight lines, each line beginning with the next letter in alphabetical order.

In other words, even though we can't see it in English translations, each of the first eight lines (verses) begins with the Hebrew letter *aleph*, which corresponds to our letter *A*.

Lines 9–16 begin with the letter *beth*, equivalent to our letter *B*, and so on. Because the subject matter of Psalm 119 is the Word of God, we might title this alphabetical acrostic poem "God's Word: The *A* to *Z* of It."

See how the modern acrostic poem that follows uses those basic elements.

JOYCE K. ELLIS

In Praise of My Eternally Faithful Jehovah

An acrostic praise psalm

Just as the sun comes up
morning after morning,
whether clouds obscure its brilliance
or clear skies frame its glory in royal blue,

Even so, Your faithfulness dawns
over Your handiwork in my heart,
banishing doubt's darkness
that descends night after night in the soul.

Heaven need not tell me day after day
the sun still shines above the clouds,
so why, my heart, do you require such proof
that your Creator still cares?

Of victories granted
and peace given and health restored
my soul could sing hour after hour,
for Jehovah keeps showing me His might.

Vows to remember, I make time after time,
yet new battles, fears, and illness clamor,
erasing memory banks of all that could cheer.

All the forgetfulness that distorts reality,
can never diminish Your unfailing love poured
over me, into me, around me, and through me,
for moment after moment, Faithful is Your name.

How great is my eternally faithful God,
who year after year erects monuments
of His steadfast love in my heart.
Praise His precious name!
—Joyce K. Ellis

My Heart's Desire

May the joy of the Lord be my strength
May the words of my mouth only edify
May God's praise fill my thoughts
May my actions bring Him praise
May my motives be pure in all I do

May the Love of the Lord move my heart
May my spirit reflect His servant attitude
May I see with His eyes
May I hear with His ears
May I never forget why I'm still here

May the truth of the Lord be my Rock
May I turn deaf ears to the Enemy
May integrity reign in my heart
May I never bring my Savior shame
May my life be transformed by His Word.
—Joyce K. Ellis

[Jesus said,] "Walk with me and work with me—watch how I do it. Learn the unforced rhythms of grace."
—Matthew 11:29 (MSG)

30

POSTLUDE: JOINING TIMELY, TIMELESS PRAISE

*From eternity to eternity
the Lord's faithful love is toward those
who fear Him,
and His righteousness toward the grandchildren.*
—Psalm 103:17 (HCSB)

From time to time, my husband and I go cemetery walking. We especially like centuries-old graveyards. We started this practice when I was doing research for a historical novel (one I hope to get back to one of these days). And we became fascinated with the words inscribed on headstones.

On the day we lowered my dad's casket into the ground next to my mother's grave, I looked at nearby headstones. A couple of rows over, among other veterans' graves at Fort Snelling National

Cemetery, something sitting atop one of the white, marble headstones, caught my eye: the face of a watch—with the hands removed. Most of my life revolves around pressure-packed deadlines. So a handless watch is a perfect dream. Here's a futuristic anecdote of my imagination:

My eyes open, and the first thing I see is the face of Jesus. Later, I will notice the incredible beauty around me, but right now, all I want is a big hug from the One who loves me more than I can ever comprehend.

And there Jesus is. Inches away from me. His arms outstretched, waiting to pull me in. He hugs me tightly—a long embrace that says He's been waiting so long for me to be there at home with Him.

I look into His face and can't take my eyes off Him. Tears flow, but He dries them with his fingers. My chronic pains melt away. My broken heart mends. He has brought me safely home. I'm in His arms. What more could I ask? All I want to do is praise Him! I drop to my knees.

What will I say? What will I sing?

In our imaginations, we can peek into eternity future via the book of Revelation and hear hymn psalms we ourselves may be singing in heaven someday:

Holy, holy, holy is the Lord God,
the Almighty—
the one who always was, who is, and
who is still to come ...
You are worthy, O Lord our God,
to receive glory and honor and power.
For you created all things,
and they exist because you created
what you pleased.
—Revelation 4:8, 11

Notice the attributes of God the following future psalms extol, the reasons for praise as well as what we owe our mighty Creator and Redeemer, the Lord Jesus Christ:

You are worthy ...
For you were killed, and by your sacrificial death you
bought for God
people from every tribe, language, nation,
and race ...
The Lamb who was killed is worthy
to receive power, wealth, wisdom,
and strength,
honor, glory, and praise!
—Revelation 5:9, 12 (GNT)

Our God is so great that in all of eternity we could never begin to cover all the reasons He deserves our praise, nor could we begin to give Him all the praise He deserves.

In my journal, instead of simply recording activities or even feelings, as in a diary, I talk through these events and emotions with the Lord on paper. He is my constant companion and the One who knows me better than anyone else. And He's ultimately the only One who can help me through the tough times—or do anything about them.

It is becoming more and more natural to bring my fears and concerns to Him and to praise Him not only for what He has done for me but also for who He is. Recording this communication regularly—and then drawing from these journals to write psalms of various genres—has helped me disentangle my thoughts and has taken me deeper and deeper in my relationship with Him.

I confess, sometimes I long for the watch hands of time to be removed. I can't wait to step into my Savior's embrace. However, I yield to *His* time. As my grandma used to say, "Every day I wake up, I realize the Lord must still have some things for me to do." And praising Him here is definitely one of them.

How exciting to think that *our* words of praise can join with those of countless believers over centuries, creating a mighty chorus of adoration to our eternal, Most-High God. So we can pray,

Oh, Incomparable Lord,
You deserve all the praise we can offer—forever and ever.
So please help us open our hearts
and let our worship flow out always—for eternity.

Journal Prompts

Scripture's psalms are songs. And songs have time signatures at the beginning of the musical score (two numbers, one stacked on the other). That designation helps musicians sing or play the piece in the tempo the composer intended. In our timely, timeless praise of God, we can write in time signatures past, present, and future.

> **Past:** We can express our feelings to God about the Red Sea moments He has already brought us through.
> **Present:** We can praise God for what He is currently teaching us as we learn to live in the "unforced rhythms of grace" (Matthew 11:29 MSG).
> **Future:** We can promise our enduring praise to God throughout our lifetime and for the entirety of eternity.

My prayer is that you will find great delight in writing the psalms of your heart—for your heart's joy, for your heart's healing, and for the glory of the One who *owns* your heart.

JOYCE K. ELLIS

Home

I wish I were home today where I belong
Back in my Father's arms
Home, where all the angels sing
Home, and safe from harm.

I wish I were home today where I belong
Basking in His radiant grace
Home, where I sit at Jesus' feet
And know I am in my place.

I wish I were home today where I belong
Where all that is wonderful is
The Home of my heart, the Home of my hope
The Home of my dreams and His.

I wish I were Home today where I belong.
Don't you wish that, like me?
Home, where our reality and joy will live
throughout eternity.
—Linnea Fellows

*May my last breath here
and my first breath there
be ones of praise
to You, O Alpha and Omega.*[80]
—Linnea Fellows

Appendix
Quick Reference:
Potential Patterns for Your Psalms

Confession psalms (patterned after Psalm 51)
    cry for mercy
    call sin sin (specificity)
    admit our sin nature
    acknowledge God's holiness
    repent
    seek cleansing and restored relationship
    profess confidence in God
    promise God our praise

Note:
A general lament psalm voices my complaint against God, seeks relief. A confession psalm acknowledges His complaint about me, seeks a restored relationship.

Confidence psalms (variable patterns, can include these common elements)
    affirmation of trust/the trustworthiness of God
    reasons for confidence
    reality of crisis or fearful things
    assurance of God's presence
    promise of future help/eternal hope

Creation psalms (patterned after Psalm 8)
    direct address to God
    general statement of praise (front bookend)
    God's supremacy and greatness
    specific illustrations from nature
    contrast of human frailty
    gift of dignity God bestows on us
    human supremacy over the rest of creation
    identical statement of praise (as v. 1)
    direct address to God
    generalized statement of praise (back bookend)

Lament psalms
    Help!
    Enough!
    I trust you.
    I choose to praise You,
    or
    Please listen to me, God.
    I can't take any more of this.
    Here's how I'm feeling:
    I'm letting it all spill out.
    I need You, Lord.
    I still believe You care
    (no matter how impossible
    things may seem right now).

Praise or Hymn psalms
    Introduction or call to praise:
        Examples:
        Great is the Lord, and most worthy of praise
        Come praise the Lord with me
        Hallelujah
        Praise the Lord
    Body: Here's why—reasons to praise, usually beginning with the words *for* or *because*
    Restatement of call to praise or further words of praise (optional)

Praise and Thanksgiving psalms (contrasted with laments)

Lament psalm may say	Thanksgiving psalm may says
	Praise the Lord
Help!	I cried out for help
Enough!	This is how bad it was
I trust You	I trusted You; You did it
I choose to praise You	I promised to praise You, so I praise You now

Wisdom psalms (variable patterns)

The following common motifs can help us structure our own wisdom psalms as we reflect on what we're learning from God.

- *blessing*
- *warning*
- *direct address to reader* (e.g., *consider, observe*)

Reminder about lament roots: Many biblical scholars believe that wisdom psalms find their roots in laments. But instead of complaining about the wicked prospering, for example, the writer reminds his hearers or readers that God is going to win in the end, and the wicked won't be so cocky then.

Just as a thanksgiving psalm can work its way beyond lament to praise, a wisdom psalm takes a step further and becomes a teacher, demonstrating what we can learn after crossing over to the other bank of the river of trouble.

Alternative wisdom psalm pattern

Psalms scholar Claus Westermann proposes this structure based on Psalm 49:

summons to hear
wisdom
question
question answered
but (*turning point/Picardy Third,* my addition)
certainty of being heard[81]

Notes

1. J. Oswald Sanders, *Enjoying Intimacy with God* (Grand Rapids: Discovery House, 2000), 58.

2. I love this rendering from the 1996 edition of the New Living Translation.

3. In his broadcasts Dr. Swindoll often uses this expression, inspired by the following quotation, "Thoughts disentangle passing o'er the lips," found in *The 7 Laws of Teaching*, by John Milton Gregory (Grand Rapids: Baker, 1962), page 55. Chuck Swindoll has disentangled his thoughts by journaling, and he encourages others to learn what journaling can do for them too. www.insight.org.

4. Chris Tiegreen, *The One Year® Hearing His Voice Devotional* (Carol Stream: Tyndale, 2014), 28.

5. Robert Sadler with Marie Chapian, *The Emancipation of Robert Sadler* (Minneapolis: Bethany, 1975), 18.

6. Chris Tiegreen, *The One-Year® Experiencing the Presence of God Devotional* (Carol Stream: Tyndale, 2011), August 9 entry.

7. "O Love That Wilt No [sic] Let Me Go," by George Matheson, The story behind the hymn. Crich Baptist Church, Derbyshire, UK, https://

www.crichbaptist.org/articles/christian-poetry-hymns/poems-hymns/o-love-that-wilt-not-let-me-go-george-matheson/.

8. Eugene H. Peterson, *The Message: Psalms* (Colorado Springs: NavPress, 1994), 4.

9. Edwin Robertson, *Dietrich Bonhoeffer's Meditations on Psalms* (Grand Rapids: Zondervan, 2002), 147.

10. Billy Graham, *The Secret of Happiness* (Nashville: Thomas Nelson, 2002), 4.

11. Charles Spurgeon, *Faith's Checkbook* (CreateSpace, 2018), 36.

12. Luci Shaw, *The Crime of Living Cautiously* (Downer's Grove: InterVarsity Press, 2005), 45.

13. Shaw, 48.

14. Max Lucado, *You'll Get Through This* (Nashville: Thomas Nelson, 2013), 10.

15. This psalm began as a free-verse poem, which originally appeared in *Scope* magazine, August 1979, page 11 and also appeared in my book *The 500 Hats of a Modern-Day Woman, Updated and Revised Edition* (Minneapolis: Encourage, 2013), 110–111. It is repeated here to illustrate the turning-point concept.

16. Arthur W. Pink, *The Wisdom of Arthur W. Pink, Vol I* (Radford, VA: Wilder Publications, 2009), 440.

17. Tiegreen, November 25 entry.

18. Dwight L. Moody, *To the Work! Exhortations to Christians* (Chicago: Moody, 1884), 39.

19. Chris Tiegreen, *One-Year® Experiencing God's Presence Devotional* (Carol Stream: Tyndale, 2011), November 16 entry.

20. Horatio G. Spafford, "It Is Well with My Soul," Public domain.

21. C. S. Lewis, *Reflections on the Psalms* (New York: Harcourt Brace Jovanovich, 1958), 94–95.

22. I've also seen this attributed to a German proverb, to Johann Wolfgang von Goethe, and others. Obviously a lot of people believe it's true. http://www.searchquotes.com/search/A_Joy_Shared/#ixzz5WmQLhlSX.

23. Read this story in 1 Samuel 21:11–22:2. There, King Abimelech is called King Achish.

24. "Salutation" by Luci Shaw, *Polishing the Petoskey Stone* (Wheaton: Shaw, 1990), 126. Used by permission of the author.

25. Joseph Bayly, *Psalms of My Life* (Colorado Springs: Victor/Cook, 1987, 2000), 23. Used by permission.

26. C. S. Lewis, *The Problem of Pain* (New York: HarperCollins, 2001), 91.

27. Randy Newman with Lin Johnson, "How to Gripe in the Spirit," *Discipleship Journal*, Issue 83 (September/October 1994): 30.

28. Don Wyrtzen, *A Musician Looks at the Psalms* (Nashville: Broadman & Holman, 2004), 91.

29. Dietrich Bonhoeffer, *Christmas Sermons* (Grand Rapids: Zondervan, 2005), 20.

30. Chris Tiegreen, *The Wonder of Advent Devotional: Experiencing the Love and Glory of the Christmas Season* (Carol Stream: Tyndale, 2017), 42.

31. The phrase "accepted in the Beloved" (in God's Beloved Son, the Lord Jesus Christ) is from the King James translation of Ephesians 1:6.

32. Leslie Brandt, *Psalms Now* (St. Louis: Concordia, 1974), 29.

33. Lucado, *You'll Get Through This*, 97.

34. I love this rendering from the 1996 edition of the New Living Translation of the Bible.

35. Luci Shaw, 30.

36. Corrie ten Boom, *Jesus Is Victor* (Old Tappan: Revell, 1984), 142.

37. Corrie ten Boom, *Clippings from My Notebook* (Nashville: Thomas Nelson, 1982), 33.

38. ten Boom, *Clippings*, 33.

39. Jane Rubietta, *Worry Less So You Can Live More* (Minneapolis: Bethany, 2015), 18.

40. Ronald B. Allen, *And I Will Praise Him: A Guide to Worship in the Psalms* (Grand Rapids: Kregel, 1992), 239.

41. Jean Sophia Pigott, "Jesus, I Am Resting, Resting," public domain.

42. Newman and Johnson, 30.

43. William Smith, *Smith's Bible Dictionary* (Westwood: Revell, 1967), 585.

44. Dallas Willard, *The Divine Conspiracy* (New Your: HarperCollins, 1998), 149.

45. James Limburg, *Psalms for Sojourners* (Minneapolis: Augsburg, 1986), 41–42.

46. Bayly, 52. Used by permission.

47. Philip Yancey, *Reaching for the Invisible God* (Grand Rapids: Zondervan, 2000), 42.

48. I've heard and seen this quote—or words like it—attributed to various other people, but it means more to me, having heard it from my loving, godly grandfather so many years ago.

49. Lucado, *You'll Get Through This*, 7.

50. C. Hassell Bullock, *Encountering the Book of Psalms* (Grand Rapids: Baker Academic, 2001), 160.

51. Ron Klug, *How to Keep a Spiritual Journal* (Minneapolis: Augsburg, 2002), 45.

52. Tim Stafford, *Knowing the Face of God* (Eugene, OR: Wipf & Stock, 2005), 62.

53. Roger C. Palms, *Enjoying the Closeness of God* (Minneapolis: World Wide Publications, 1989), 61.

54. Don Wyrtzen, *A Musician Looks at the Psalms* (Nashville: Broadman & Holman, 2004), 153.

55. C. S. Lewis, *Mere Christianity* (New York: HarperCollins, 2009), 123.

56. Walter Brueggemann, *The Message of the Psalms* (Minneapolis, Augsburg, 1984), 97.

57. Dietrich Bonhoeffer, ed. Edwin H. Robertson, *Voices in the Night* (Grand Rapids: Zondervan, 1999), 65.

58. "Pastor Joe Wright's Prayer," http://www.eaec.org/desk/joe_wright_prayer.htm. Used by permission.

59. David Egner, "Why Can't I Feel Forgiven?" *Our Daily Bread Online*, January 27, 1987, https://odb.org/1997/01/27/why-cant-i-feel-forgiven/.

60. adapted from the article "Legal Wrangling" by Joyce K. Ellis, which originally appeared in *Indeed* 14, no. 3 (May/June 2014).

61. Gayle Roper, "I Can't Forgive Myself," *Discipleship Journal*, Issue 99 (May/June 1997): 30.

62. David Daniels, "True Confession," *Discipleship Journal*, Issue 99 (May/June 1997): 68.

63. Daniels, 69.

64. Timothy Keller with Kathy Keller, *The Songs of Jesus* (New York: Viking, 2015), 336.

65. Erwin W. Lutzer, *Failure: the Back Door to Success* (Chicago: Moody, 2016), 99.

66. Lutzer, 18.

67. Charles R. Swindoll, *Three Steps Forward, Two Steps Back* (Nashville: Thomas Nelson, 1980), 115.

68. Watchman Nee, *Praising*, Living Stream Ministry, https://www.ministrybooks.org/books.cfm?id=22E3DF. Scripture quotation in line 6 is from Psalm 23:4 (KJV).

69. Ravi Zacharias and Vince Vitale, *Why Suffering?* (New York: FaithWords, 2015), 182.

70. Zacharias and Vitale, 183.

71. Saint Augustine, Henry Chadwick, *Confessions* (Oxford: Oxford University, 2009), 3.

72. Dr. Paul Brand and Philip Yancey, *Fearfully and Wonderfully Made* (Grand Rapids: Zondervan, 1997), 40.

73. Charles Spurgeon, *Faith's Checkbook* (New Kensington: Whitaker, 1843), 143.

74. J. Oswald Sanders, *Enjoying Intimacy with God* (Grand Rapids: Discovery House, 2000), 17.

75. According to biblical languages scholar Dr. Theron Young, in personal correspondence with the author, *Kum ba ya*, not a biblical phrase, actually comes from the Aramaic, and it means, "Arise, come, Lord."

76. J. Oswald Sanders, *Dynamic Spiritual Leadership* (Grand Rapids: Discovery House, 1999), 170–171.

77. Charles R. Swindoll, *Living the Psalms: Encouragement for the Daily Grind* (Brentwood: Worthy, 2012), 221–222.

78. Based on outline by biblical scholar Claus Westermann, *The Psalms: Structure, Content and Message* (Minneapolis: Augsburg, 1980), 113–114.

79. original psalm appeared in *Family Life Today* magazine, September 1983: 50.

80. from a confession psalm Linnea Fellows shared with the author. Used by permission.

81. Westermann.

Praise the Lord forever!
Amen and amen!
—Psalm 89:52